INTELLIGENCE

ITS ORGANIZATION AND DEVELOPMENT

INTELLIGENCE

ITS ORGANIZATION
AND DEVELOPMENT

MICHAEL CUNNINGHAM

The Moore School of Electrical Engineering
University of Pennsylvania
Philadelphia, Pennsylvania

 1972   ACADEMIC PRESS   New York and London

ACADEMIC PRESS, INC.
111 Fifth Avenue, New York, New York 10003

United Kingdom Edition published by
ACADEMIC PRESS, INC. (LONDON) LTD.
24/28 Oval Road, London NW1 7DD

LIBRARY OF CONGRESS CATALOG CARD NUMBER: 76-187223

PRINTED IN THE UNITED STATES OF AMERICA

For Emma

CONTENTS

PREFACE

Psychology, indeed any science, is an elephant under investigation by a group of blind men, each with a hand on a different one of the poor beast's members, and each hopeful that the particular member in his hand represents the essence of the whole. All of which is a fine and reasonable way of investigating a very large and complex thing (except when hopes run too high or the blind men consider one another fools). My own modest contribution to this group grope project is a bit different in that I have tried to show how some of the members might be connected.

The theory presented in this book was devised in preparation for a computer reproduction of intelligent learning behavior, and as such should be of interest to both psychologist and to those computer scientists interested in intelligence. The intended use of the theory has perhaps had as much effect on the nature of the theory as the input information from which it was fashioned. Several bodies of psychological knowledge and theory have been reorganized and synthesized into a single model that is amenable to rapid, simple, and efficient computation. The cell assembly theory of Hebb has been simplified to its bare essentials, and Piaget's theory of the development of sensorimotor intelligence has been made more concrete and explicit. Such concepts as drive and reinforcement have been subsumed by the inclusion of the orienting and defense responses as variable controls on channel capacity. The union of these several theories and bodies of knowledge is, I believe, sufficiently interesting to merit attention. And at least one of Gray's (1964) stringent criteria for publication has been met.

I owe a great debt to the people who have taught me and encouraged me and paved my way. A mention of their names here is puny reward for their time

and patience, but probably more than they expected. They are Irving Lazar of
the Appalachian Commission whose early and continuing help made this book
possible; Professors John Weir and Frederick Thompson with whom I worked on
my first computerized model of psychological development at Caltech; Professors John W. Carr, III, Harry Gray, and Philip Salapatec who worked with me
and guided me in the development of the present model at the University of
Pennsylvania; David T. Lykken of the University of Minnesota and Sheldon
White of Harvard University who helped with the process of publication. I also
appreciate the help of Bob Ritenhour and Larry Doig at EG&G in Las Vegas
who helped several times with the manuscript and presentation.

Finally, the work on this book and some of the early investigations that
led up to it were supported by the U.S. Army Electronics Command at Fort
Monmouth through contract DA 28-043-AMC-02377(E) and the Public Health
Service through research grant MH-19201 from the National Institute of Mental
Health.

The quotations from Ruth Weir's book *Language in the Crib* are with the
kind permission of her publishers Mouton & Co.

Michael Cunningham

CHAPTER I
AN APPROACH TO THE PROBLEM

Introduction

The aim of this book is to develop a formalized approach to intelligence—one that is sufficiently precise and abstract to allow a working model to be built on present day computers, but that is also sufficiently flexible and factual to allow an interpretation and unification of some of the findings and concepts of psychology. We will begin at a level of organization that roughly corresponds to the cell assemblies postulated by Hebb (1949). The cell assembly is a group of neurons which have become interconnected as a result of experience and which thereafter tend to function sometimes as a single unit. The orienting and defense responses emphasized in Russian psychology ever since Pavlov's (1927) work will be formalized as a control system superimposed on the cell assemblies. Here the work of Sokolov (1963) is particularly useful, as his "neural model" of a sensory event seems a ready analogue of the cell assembly. Using this updated cell assembly model, the developmental psychology of very early childhood as studied by Piaget (1936) will be traced in an attempt to show the remarkable congruence between the two. Then, tentative interpretations will be made for a number of psychological issues of recent concern. Finally, a computer test and implementation will be outlined.

The Building Block and Black Box Approaches: Neurons
or Integrated Behavior?

In terms of the level of organization, there are two extremes to the modeling and theorizing about intelligence. Most work is done at one or another of these extremes. I will call these two approaches the *building block approach* and the *black box approach.* A brief discussion of the typical features and difficulties of these approaches or levels of organization may be useful in stirring interest in a compromise between the two.

The building block approach to the modeling of intelligence begins at a low level of organization by considering, usually, the individual neuron which seems to be the smallest indivisible and easily observable functioning unit of the brain. An understanding of the neuron must therefore be essential to an understanding of the brain and its activity. To this end, a vast accumulation of knowledge about the neuron, its functioning, and its connections to other neurons has been piled up. Most psychological models of sensory perception are neuron models [a good example of which is Dodwell's (1964) work on the visual system]. And, of course, the whole of neurophysiology must be included here. Generally, any model that involves complexes built up out of many similar elements I am classifying here as a building block model; associations, memories, and concepts are other forms of building blocks.

As a specific example of the building block approach, neuron models try to understand and simulate the functioning of an idealized neuron in a network of similar neurons. These models range from attempts to simulate the observed activity and structure of an actual living neuron network (the work reported by Moreno-Diaz, 1965, is an example of this) to the use of electronic circuitry to represent an abstracted and idealized neuron as in Rosenblatt's (1962) work. Some models try to simulate the more automatic "wired-in" features of a complex system such as the retina, and other models try to account for developmental features like learning and memory. By firing some of the neurons in the network, input is given, and by monitoring the firing of other neurons, the output of the network is taken. In effect, some neurons are made to "grow" connections or at least change their relationship to other neurons, depending upon the use or experience of the network, upon the series of inputs it has already had. Starting off with a good deal of prewiring of a certain form, the aim of a simulation of a neuron model is to discover if a given pattern of inputs results in some theoretically predicted pattern of outputs. As a rule, each neuron model and, more generally, any building block model has three distinct parts: a functional theory about the operation of the basic building blocks, a structural theory about the way these building blocks are joined to make a network, and a developmental theory about how the building blocks and their interconnections are changed by experience.

Neuron models on the computer have been successful in pattern recognition experiments, and have even been put to use in applications. Precise mathematical generalizations such as Nilsson's (1965) have been used to describe the results of the simpler networks; in cases where we know the mathematics apply, we may even be able to guarantee successful recognition after a certain amount of training. Unfortunately, these pure neuron models have not been able to learn how to use the recognized patterns to build new patterns of output and to recognize new composite patterns of input. They cannot construct hierarchies of patterns. They seem incapable of any sort of planning or manipulation of what they have learned; they are passively input dependent. We can even increase their size and we only seem to get finer discriminations but no new capacity for dealing with these discriminations once made. And for the sake of analysis and applicability of mathematical generalizations, models are only a few neurons thick from input to output. All this reflects a general failing of building block models—they often seem unable to advance beyond a certain level of complexity. Either the theorist breaks down under the burden of details, or the increasing complexity of the structure ceases to give qualitatively different results. The original construction principle, or the building block, or the theorist himself is not strong enough to achieve the complexity desired.

The black box approach to the modeling of intelligence starts at a high level of organization where the microscopic operating details of the elements of the model are largely ignored and attention is focused on the handling of input and output information by an overall system. The basic premise here is that observation of an intelligent human involved in some activity such as memorizing lists, playing chess, solving problems, or just making discriminations, should enable us to figure out what it is that he is doing and simulate this—even if we are entirely ignorant of the exact method he is using to encode information and operate on it. At least we should be able to describe his activities with parameters, measure these, and invent information processing systems that give the same values for the parameters as those measured from the human subject. The concepts we use to construct our information processing system often come from (perhaps unexamined) outside sources—the English language, our intuition, biology, neurophysiology, or the computer sciences. However, once the black box model is built and tested, the better the values of the parameters match between the model and the subject, the more certain we are that the model indeed reflects some psychological reality. In psychology, black box models are used most in exploring behavioral evidence of the structure and function of memory and motivation. I would include here such theories as Bruner's (1966), the Gestalt theories, and much of the recent work in language and grammars.

To take a specific example area, in problem solving, what the subject is often doing is making more or less justified guesses using rules of thumb whose results are uncertain, but surprisingly often effective. These guesses often involve not merely possible solutions or operations on data, but whole strategies or programs of operations. Consciously used operations, strategies, and rules of thumb are reportable, observable, definable, and programmable on a computer. They may range from simply guessing what input data should be looked at, to trying out complex transformations on the data and putting it in a more recognizable or useful form. They usually involve planning of goals and their prerequisite subgoals, keeping track of failures and successes, searching for certain kinds of data, and matching up data with applicable operations. All these problem solving activities are black box level activities in that we can use them in many different information processing systems regardless of the exact methods of encoding and transforming information; we can discern these activities in the sequence of input and output produced by the human subject even though we are ignorant of the internal workings between input and output.

Computer models of problem solving are successful in solving the tasks set before them, but rarely does a machine made to solve one problem succeed on another, even though the other problem has been solved by some other computer model. In a similar way, many psychological concepts are successful only in explaining very limited phenomena. Rarely does a theory of short term memory have more than an incidental remark to make about motivation, for example. This reflects a general failing of the black box approach. In building a black box model, we are usually ignorant (and oftentimes proud of it) of the internal working of what we are modeling. As a result, the model we build is only an ad hoc simulation whose internal workings are of questionable psychological validity; applied in another situation, the model is a failure without additional ad hoc alterations.

In summary, the building block or neuron models seem unable to advance upward; they can be organized to recognize input patterns, but they cannot achieve a sufficient complexity to rearrange these patterns into superpatterns or common subpatterns—concepts never develop in a neuron model. Neuron nets alone cannot focus attention on the relations between patterns. They have only a vague and general "awareness" of all the current inputs and of the local conditions in each of the neurons; no one pattern can be concentrated upon and manipulated much differently from the others. The alerting and drive functions usually attributed to the brain stem are not included. Somewhere, some vital organizing principle beyond simply hooking up neurons has been overlooked. On the other hand, the black box models seem unable to advance downward; that their constructs represent anything in reality is often uncertain. Black box models can only operate with certain classes of patterns—they are not general enough. Given a new set of patterns of input-output behavior from a different problem area (say a chess playing machine given a problem in logic), they never become capable of handling it. At some level below that penetrated by an input-output analysis there seems to lurk an organizing principle that remains independent of specific classes of input patterns. There is something in the internal workings that is independent of the information handled, and the black box approach misses it.

Alas, the two kinds of models (or schools of thought) seem rarely to come together to compensate each others failings. A few notable efforts in that direction have been made. An example is that of Deutsch (1960) who constructed something of a hybrid theory using building blocks of neural analyzers and a black box concept of drive or motive. Dodwell's (1964) theory of vision is a black box model, but the information processing system used is carefully built within the framework of neuron nets (as they are understood from sources external to Dodwell's experiments and observations). Perhaps the best known attempt to bring the neuron building-block level high enough to explain the whole black box is that of Hebb (1949).

Joining the Two Approaches

Twenty years ago, Hebb (1949) first presented his theory of the assembly of neurons, basing his work on the neurophysiology of Lorente de Nó (1938). Working from Lorente de Nó's description of the interactions of neurons, Hebb constructed theoretical assemblies of neurons, and using these assemblies, gave interpretations of many behavioral facts. The cell assembly was a group of neurons which could function as a unit and which could act to form new assemblies or could recombine into groupings, subgroupings, and supergroupings of assemblies. The assembly represented the internal coding of learned information—of sensory perceptions, of motor skills, and of the thought processes themselves. Even before Hebb, but working from the observed behavior of children, and using Baldwin's (1895) idea of circular reaction between the individual and the environment, Piaget (1936) began to develop his theory of schemata and the assimilation and accommodation which recombined old schemata into new ones. Thus, with both Hebb's physiological building block approach and with Piaget's behavioral black box approach, we come to what is perhaps the heart of the matter—some representation whose elements can be recombined indefinitely into higher and higher orders of structure. Furthermore, these elements are not merely passive records; indeed, they call each other into action, and through the senses and motor outputs, they incorporate the outside world into the developing internal world. A brief description of the central features of Hebb's neural model and Piaget's behavioral model is useful here.

The *cell assemblies* of Hebb were groups of neurons excited by patterns of sensory and motor activity. With repeated presentation of a pattern of activity, excited neurons formed themselves into a cell assembly in which neural activity subsequently reverberated in the presence of the now learned patterns of activity. Reverberation meant the cell assembly could maintain the excitation of its individual neurons for some time after the arousing sensory and motor activity had ceased; excitation circulates back and forth among the neurons of the cell assembly. Furthermore, a pattern of activity from old reverberating assemblies could cause the formation of new derived assemblies which later are aroused by reverberations in the old assemblies. These new higher order assemblies were thus at least one step removed from the direct influence of sensory input. In the course of learning, assemblies would be linked together and new assemblies created to form networks of assemblies which directed, and more or less were, the central thought processes. Passage of reverberations from an active set of assemblies to another set of assemblies, defined a sort of stream of consciousness or train of thought, a phase sequence as Hebb called it. Current sensory inputs plus the activity of already reverberating assemblies would determine which new assemblies, if any, would next be aroused to reverberation.

The "meaning" of a structure of assemblies would be the other structures it might be able to excite: sometimes one, sometimes another, depending on the overall activity of other assemblies in the nervous system. The prompt one-shot learning typical of adults was dependent upon the earlier organization of the relevant assemblies. A perception would be an irregularly recurring phase sequence or cycle of activity within a complex of assemblies. A train of thought would be a series of such cycles. Different phase sequences or series of reverberations in different assemblies would branch off on different paths; sensory input could disrupt, reinforce, or be neutral to one or another sequence of neural activity. An interacting complex of cycles could maintain interest, but this is an unstable interest that could shift about a core of cycles relevant to whatever was being thought about. In short, these assemblies and the structures formed from them were the central nervous system's representation of the outside world, and their reverberation represented the nervous system's functioning.

The *schemata* of Piaget were theoretical constructs—hypothetical building blocks—based upon the observation of behavior. A schema was a more or less integrated pattern of behavior including the motor output acts, the sensory inputs from objects or actions associated with that behavior, and presumably any unobservable structures or activities of the central nervous system associated with the behavior. The early inborn schemata formed circular reactions with the body and with objects in the outside world; a schema acting on an object through motor outputs was itself further excited by the sensory inputs in turn being aroused by the object. One schema might include or assimilate another schema's functioning to itself. At the same time, the other schema might change or accommodate itself to fit the functioning of the first. For example, the schema of the eye might activate the schema of the hand and so cause motion of an observed object. Objects of the outside world could themselves be assimilated or accommodated by a schema insofar as the objects were represented by sensory inputs from them or motor activity applied to them. Schemata could activate subordinate schemata, they could direct the activity of other schemata, they could interact with the objects of the world. The changes in a schema through assimilation and accommodation represented learning, seemingly slow at first, but later more rapid and directed as increasingly complex generalized schemata developed. There were primarily sensory schemata (of recognition), motor schemata (of skills), and internal schemata (of formal and concrete operations). These schemata are representations which can freely recombine to form new ones and can direct the overall activity of the system. Like Hebb, Piaget envisioned a flexible and interactive representation of the outside world. In addition, Piaget supposed there was an overall process called equilibration that controlled the assimilations and accommodations of all the individual schemata.

Hebb's (1949) theory is very much a building block theory. The exact nature of the cell assembly is carefully explained functionally, structurally, and developmentally; and the entire function of the processes of intelligence are presumed to be in terms of the cell assemblies. Piaget's (1936) theory is very much a black box. Although the schemata are a form of building block, their exact nature is not explained; rather, they are presumed to be definable by the complex behavior patterns of input and output which they control and their function and development is presumed to be controled by the higher processes of assimilation, accommodation, and equilibration. However, there are a number of ways in which Hebb's neural building blocks and Piaget's behavioral building blocks are similar. To give a quick preview of what lies ahead, it is through this similarity of their building blocks that Hebb's and Piaget's theories can be unified. And, in the process of unification, the work of Sokolov (1963) will be incorporated to update Hebb and give a neurological interpretation of Piaget's process of equilibration.

The assemblies and the schemata are both just theoretical constructs, deriving from two widely different points of view, but with several common characteristics which must be fundamental to a successful description of the intelligence which is in the central nervous system. It is, I think, these characteristics, however arrived at, that give the two theories their power to describe the intelligent processes:

anarchical hierarchy—there are structures, and substructures, and superstructures, each level formed from structures of the lower level, but all operating by the same rules, and in the end being the same thing; there is diversity of structure but unity of function;

generality—the processes of development and function are independent of the "meaning" of the sensory input or motor output; they function the same for all forms of input and output;

interaction—the basic building blocks of the model can call each other into
   action and affect each other's activity; in the same way they can interact
   with the objects of the external world;
functional representation—the elements themselves are the units of coding for
   the experience with the world at the same time that they are units of the
   system's internal functioning; the unit of information and of operation is
   the same.

What I have attempted in this book is a unification and expansion of
Hebb's (1949), Piaget's (1936), and Sokolov's (1963) observations and theories.
Assuming the physical existence of something akin to the cell assembly, I will
start at that level of organization—somewhere in the middle between neurons
and behavioral systems. The result will be a hybrid theory with cell assemblies as
building blocks and with a monitoring system for regulation and control.
Hopefully, the new theory presented here will have some psychological validity
(even without test and verification) in so far as the model will be a formalization
and systemization of Hebb's assemblies, of Piaget's schemata, and of Sokolov's
cognitive reflexes.

The plan of this book is essentially as follows: first, a bit of formalism—
abstract nonsense, an empty basket—is introduced to give us a way of collecting,
representing, and talking about the discoveries we are going to make. At the
same time, a good deal of Hebb's underlying neurophysiology is quietly
included, to give weight. Then, in the next chapter, the early development of
human intelligence is traced, using Piaget's astute observations. While this is
being done, the formalism will be filled out—an information processing model
along Hebb's lines (as updated by Sokolov's work) will be made of Piaget's
observations. This is the unified model promised earlier. In the rest of the
chapters a few translations are made into the unified model's language for a
handful of traditional psychological constructs, and some studies of sight,
language, and conceptual development are interpreted in the model. An
explanation of Sokolov's observations is given. At the end, a computer
implementation is outlined.

A Formalism

In developing this model of intelligence, I have two aims in mind; one is to
have a model that reflects some psychological reality, the other is to have a
model for building computer-based systems that display some degree of
intelligence. On the one hand, we should be able to tie the model firmly to the
most accessible example of intelligence we have, the human mind. On the other
hand, we should be able to abstract this intelligence out of the specific
implementation and limitation of the brain and reinterpret it in another
medium.

To begin, we will need a formalism for talking about things. There will be two basic aspects of this formalism, the data structure of building blocks (called elements as a neutral compromise between Hebb and Piaget) and the operating system. The elements and their interconnections will be represented by the data structure, while the constraints that define how the elements function and interact with the environment will be represented by the operating system. The data structure is the growing accumulation of experience encoded into the memory and the operating system is the unchanging part of the model. The data structure roughly represents the memory system of the cerebrum and the operating system roughly represents the regulatory functions of the brain stem. The flow of nerve signals through the brain is represented by the interaction of the learned data structure and the hereditary operating system. This distinction between data structure and operating system is akin to the distinction in computer technology between software (the programs stored in memory) and hardware (the central processor and wired-in operations).

There are two aspects of the data structure that must be considered—a permanent aspect and a transitory aspect. First, there are the relatively permanent memory elements themselves which correspond to Hebb's cell assemblies and rather loosely to Piaget's schemata. Neurophysiologically, an element is any group of neurons (and perhaps associated cells such as neuroglia) in which a particular temporal and spacial firing pattern occurs that is reliably reproduceable by certain patterns of stimulation (even after long periods of inactivity). If an element includes sensory receptors it will be called an input element, and if it includes neurons which activate muscles or glands it will be called an output element. Finally, if an element is formed as a result of experience and learning, it will be called a memory element. An important part of the structure of an element involves the connections, facilitations, or links from that element to others. How does the firing pattern of one element arouse firing patterns of other elements? Clearly, some of the activity in the first element is transmitted to the other elements (perhaps by a subset of common neurons), and if the firing pattern in the first element is strong enough or supported by activity from elsewhere, the firing patterns of some of the other elements may be aroused. The associative, connected structure of memory would suggest that the facilitations or links between elements are themselves relatively stable and permanent.

The second aspect of the data structure to be considered is the relatively transitory neural activity contained in an element. Remember what defines an element is the existence of a firing pattern that is reproducible and constant from activation to activation. The problem is: what constitutes a reproduction of a certain spatial-temporal firing pattern, and, further, what is a "certain" firing pattern? We might imagine a two-dimensional graph as a representation of any one particular spatial-temporal firing pattern. The neurons of the related cell assembly could be arranged along one axis of the graph, and time could be the variable along the other axis. The firing pattern of each neuron could then be sampled and recorded for a few seconds while the cell assembly was reverberating. This would produce some pattern of dots on our graph. Since neural systems are inherently noisy, we cannot insist on an overly precise firing pattern, but might instead use such measures as cross-correlations of pairs of neurons in the cell assembly. Given all the cross-correlations of the element's consituent neurons, we could define the activity of that element at a particular time as the degree to which the cross-correlations over the last few seconds matched those of the defining firing pattern. Of course all this is operationally useless in neurophysiology; cross-correlations between two or three related neurons are difficult enough, let alone all the cells of a cell assembly. Nevertheless, as an aid to the intuition and to give concrete image to our conceptions, cross-correlations of hundreds of individual neuron firing patterns are useful. It turns out to be even more useful, in making simulations and actual computations, to assume that the presence of a particular spatial-temporal firing pattern may be characterized by a single transitory parameter—called here the activity—and that the facilitations passed along the links to other elements is a simple function of this overall activity.

Corresponding to the division between transitory activity and permanent structure in the cell assembly, there are two aspects of the formalized model. The active thought process is defined by the operating system for transforming activity from element to element. The innate sensory, motor, and reflex systems, and the long term memories of experience are defined by the data structure of elements and links.

A graphic representation of the data structure will be useful. A circle will represent an element and an arrow between two elements will represent a link from one to the other. Activity may pass along the arrow in one direction only, from the element at the tail end, to the element at the point. The first element will be said to facilitate the second. Input is represented by allowing some action of the environment to activate some of the special input elements of the model, and output is represented by performing some action on the environment when one of the special output elements of the model is sufficiently active. In a sense, there are links pointing to the input elements from certain objects in the environment, and there are links from the output elements pointing to objects in the environment. These links are external to the model and not subject to the operating system, but they serve to emphasize the continuity between data structure and environment. Viewed from within the nervous system, the rest of the body is external to the nervous system and appears as part of the environment. A graphical representation of a purely reflex system is shown in Fig. 1 (p. 14).

It may be desirable at times to consider a complex of interconnected elements as a single unit. A group of elements which are all mutually facilitating or in which activity wanders back and forth from element to element may all be considered a single element with a single overall activity. A large set of sensory input elements which tend to be activated together by the environment may be considered as a single complex input element. Again, statistical measures such as cross-correlations might be imagined, but now extending over greater time periods. Is the entire nervous system not an element with time periods extending over days and weeks? Isn't an individual neuron an element with time periods of a few hundredths of a second? Is the utterance of a single sound, a word, or a sentence caused by a single element? There is a problem in deciding just where to set the bounds of an element. The solution is to set the bounds as suits our convenience. In a very complex situation we may want to leave many details unstated. In such a case, we may encircle a whole complex and speak of it as one element, ignoring for the time its substructure of links and elements. Links from subelements to other elements not in the complex will become links from the complex element to other (perhaps complex) elements. The functioning of such a complex element will still depend on its substructure, but the rules for its development and operation are of the same general form as, and derived from, the primitive rules that apply to the subelements. The complex element will be used only as an informal aid to what would otherwise be an impossibly complex discussion.

Although I have introduced the dichotomy between data structure and operating system, in fact there is a matching duality. We might consider the data structure as a director (or even a part) of the operating system and consider complex operating systems as being built out of the elementary operating system by information in the data structure. This is precisely what is done by the electronic computer which has primitive operations that may be specified in the computer's memory or data structure. As a result, the data structure contains not merely data, but also complex series of operations or programs that may make the computer behave in the most astounding ways—ways that the computer's original designers never dreamed of. These programs may be viewed logically as complex operations and they may also be viewed as data. In our model, we might expect complex systems of thought and logic to be assimilated into the data structure through experience. The end result may be a system that is behaviorally far fetched from the very simple (but powerful) system that is genetically defined.

It is a fundamental assumption in the development of this model that there is, at some level, a small basic set of data structures and operations fixed by the hereditary organization of the brain, and that out of this initial set develops all the complex structures and operations eventually recognized as being intelligent. The level of Hebb's assemblies and of Piaget's schemata is far enough above the level of the neurons to escape the many irrelevant and the many undiscovered details of a system composed of ten billion complicated functioning units. Yet, the assembly or schema seems to be a level low enough to be completely general and descriptive of all behavior from birth. In computer design, this level might correspond to the level of registers and logic modules, as opposed to transistors and diodes at a lower level, or arithmetic operations at a higher level. It will be a great convenience to be able to begin our discussion and our computer simulation without having to specify the structure of all the elements of memory—they have not even been created by experience yet. In contrast, a neuron model must specify almost all the interconnections between all the neurons before a simulation or discussion can even get underway. And a black box model with only its input-output analysis may assume something akin to assuming that a phonograph record inside the throat produces human speech—the assumed mechanism may be wrong and fail to relate at all to intelligence, even though it explains some input-output behavior.

It is also a basic assumption of this book that we should begin with the simplest case and work our way up to a fully functioning intelligence. Thus we begin at birth where the functional characteristics of the nervous system are not hidden and confused by the structures imposed by experience. We will follow the infant through subsequent stages of development, at each stage assuming the minimum necessary to explain any newly emergent behavior not explainable in terms of the old. I will make constant reference to the excellent work of Piaget who, in *The Origins of Intelligence in Children,* follows the intellectual development of his own children through six stages from earliest exercise of the reflexes, to the first inventions through mental recombination. To understand Piaget I will be using, with a bit of updating and a little explicit reference, the precise, concrete approach of Hebb in his *The Organization of Behavior.* This will appear as a series of abstract statements used as postulates in explaining Piaget's observations and theoretical constructs.

CHAPTER 2
THE MIND OF A CHILD
(EXCEEDETH OUR UNDERSTANDING)

Stage I: Reflex Exercise; Beginning from Birth

Babies are born with a hereditary set of sensitivities connected by reflexes to motor responses. Some examples of the more specific of these reflexes are the grasping, sucking, swallowing, choking, and visual tracking reflexes. There also seem to be general arousal mechanisms which produce very pervasive changes in motor activity and physiological conditions as a result of almost any stimulation such as touch, sound, sight, or hunger pains. This initial situation will be represented in the model by two sets of elements, an input set and an output set, with links between elements of the two sets. As suggested by Fig. 1, these initial elements are on the border between the external and internal worlds. Neurologically, these elements are structures of neurons which include the sensory receptors and motor effectors of the peripheral nervous system and related neurons throughout the central nervous system. Stated in an abstract specification of the Data Structure:

DS1: The system is initially endowed with a set of *input elements* and a set of *output elements,* with links called *reflexes* from elements of the input set to elements of the output set.

Objects of the external world activate the sensory inputs, and, in turn, are affected by the activity (changed by the muscles into motion) of the output side of the system. In circular reaction, the environment transforms the signals from the output side of the nervous system and feeds new signals back into the input side; the elements of the internal data structure similarly pass or transform activity from the input to the output side of the nervous system. Since intelligence is presumably independent of the exact nature of the input-output elements, their formal description is deliberately vague:

DS2: Each element has a transitory parameter called its *activity* which is represented as a real number.

DS3: *Activity of the input elements* depends on external conditions of the environment.

DS4: *Activity of the output elements* may alter in some way the external conditions of the environment.

The problem for intelligence is to construct a functioning representation in its data structure that can interact with the external objects and support an ever continuing, ever changing and expanding circular reaction with the environment. The body itself is external to the nervous system and here is considered a part of the environment, but one that is especially close, always present, and consistent. For the sake of completeness and to emphasize that intelligence and environ-

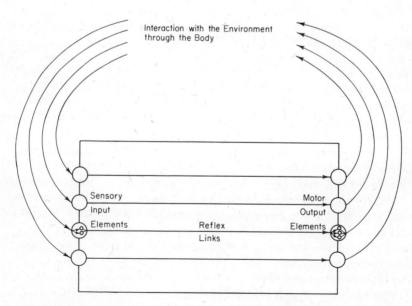

Fig. 1. A graphic representation of the data structure at stage one reflex exercise.

ment interact as a single system, links might be drawn from external objects to the sensory inputs they may activate, and other links might be drawn to the objects from motor outputs that may have effect on them.

Intuitively, the arrows may be thought of as channels of activity or information flow, through objects on the outside, and through elements on the inside. Intellectual growth is the result of an interaction between the internal elements of the nervous system, and the external objects of the environment. The data structure should develop and change so as to reflect and interact with the external objects. The structure of internal elements might be considered an epistemological representation of objects and their relationships in the environment. We only know the outer world by means of our inner structures; our own internal structure of elements is a virtual image (in terms of our sensory and motor capacities) of the structure of the objects in the environment.

We know that a great many sensory receptors and motor neurons may be involved in one reflex activity, and also that a single sensory receptor or motor neuron may in turn be involved in a great many different reflexes. From this follows some of the generalized and undifferentiated character of the infant's behavior. For convenience, a set of inputs (or outputs) with similar connections will be considered one large element so we can neglect the details when desirable. (See Fig. 1, where parts of the internal structure of some of the elements are shown.) This is not a part of the formal data structure, but will be a convention for our misuse of it. Formally, each of the smallest distinguishable and reproducable spatial-temporal firing patterns associated with sensory and motor activity should be represented by a single element in the initial data structure. But just what those patterns are is far from clear, and as irrelevant to the general nature of intelligence as the alphabet is irrelevant to the general nature of language.

Every sensory input must be reflex linked to some motor output, and vice versa. Otherwise we could never observe any behavioral evidence for their existence. At the very least, every input seems to be linked through the brain stem to certain autonomic reactions by a very general mechanism of arousal. This is an important aspect of the data structure that assures a *necessary minimum of internal connection:*

DS5: Each input must have a link pointing to at least one output and each output must be so connected to at least one input.

A sensory input or motor output not somehow linked to the opposite side may be said to be immature and nonfunctional. In the human infant, one difficult problem in developmental theory is to explain when each reflex, sense, or motor activity becomes operational, and whether this is a result of learning or of strictly internal maturation.

That there are internal maturational factors is strongly suggested by a few simple observations. One is the childish incapacity to walk or to wink one eye before a certain age. Another common observation is of the more infantile incapacity to make delicately controlled movements—an arm is either thrust out or not moved at all. Immaturity seems to consist sometimes of a simple lack of strength, and sometimes of an inability to activate a smaller rather than a larger structure. We might formalize the strictly maturational aspects of development as a gradual increase in the maximal activity that can be achieved by an input element, or as a gradual increase in the capacity of an output element to effect a movement or change in the environment:

DS6: Each input and output element has its own maximum capacity above which its activity cannot rise; this capacity may increase or *mature* with time and regardless of experience.

A remarkable thing about the reflexes is that they tend to maintain their own activity by way of external objects; they assimilate or use objects for their own functioning. Thus, once initiated, the grasping reflex tends to maintain contact with the very object in the hand that first stimulated it. The situation is similar with the sucking reflex. Reflexes tend to maintain their own activity by forming what we may call reflexive circular reactions with external objects. The sensory input from the objects starts the reflex, and the reflex output keeps the object in contact with the original sensory input, thus reproducing the reflex. This kind of automatic circular reaction exercises the reflexes and ensures their development. It requires of the data structure that:

DS7: The relation between inputs, outputs, reflex links, and the objects of the environment must be such that the objects activate and exercise the reflexes and set up *reflexive circular reactions* with them.

When this condition is not satisfied, the reflex tends to remain unchanged by experience and next to useless for the development of intelligence. Such reflexes would be the sneezing, coughing, and defense sort of reflexes. Even such a biologically important reflex as swallowing remains undifferentiated by experience and intellectually unimportant. With all these examples, automatic reflexive circular reaction is impossible because the reflex itself breaks contact with the stimulation that arouses it.

Turning now to the operating system which transforms activity from element to element, it may be observed with the more specific reflexes that whenever a sensory input is sufficiently activated by some external condition (an object pressed to the baby's hand or mouth), the corresponding motor outputs are activated through the reflex links (the baby grasps or sucks the object). This is simply a description of the *passage of neural activity* from an input to an output element and can be formalized as an Operating System specification:

OS1: Under certain conditions (described in OS2) an element with a high level of activity (that is, one with a large number for the activity parameter) may, as a function of its own activity, increase the activity of each of the other elements to which its links point. Such an element is said to *reverberate.*

If stimulation is too weak, a reflex may not be aroused at all. There seems to be a threshold above which the stimulation must rise before activity is passed along the links to other elements. This threshold varies with the state of the child, and is not so much a function of the individual elements involved, as it is a function of the overall condition of the nervous system. In particular, the successful functioning of a reflex is often observed to reduce output from other reflexes. If an infant is engaged in making reflexive movements of the arms, legs, body, or eyes, almost any object placed in the mouth, that initiates sucking, will bring almost all other activity to a halt. The introduction of small, moving, bright objects into the visual field will increase the number of scanning movements of the eyes and decrease other motor activities (even sucking may be thus suspended). Excessively strong stimulation of almost any sort will bring a halt to all motor activity except for the peculiar respiratory reflex of crying. Even sleep might be viewed in part as a reflexive circular reaction of kinesthetic feedback from relaxed musculature and output signals that keep the muscles relaxed. This "reflex" is the most effective one in blocking activity of the other reflexes. For the infant, little more than one reflex at a time may be functioning—the infant has a very small attention span in terms of the number of fully functioning (or as Hebb would say, reverberating) elements. This is formalized as:

OS2: Only a certain number of elements of greatest activity will be said to *reverberate* or pass activity on to other elements.

The *number* of reverberating elements will be called the *attention span* and the *set* of reverberating elements will be called *attention*. Note that our common English use of attention span as a length of time is not implied here.

When supporting stimulation is removed, reflex activity may continue for awhile, although it does finally cease. As an example, the infant may continue sucking movements even after the bottle is removed. Thus, it would appear that reverberations in a highly active element may continue for some time after the original activating input has stopped; there is some *time delay* in the function of the nervous system.

OS3: Once made to reverberate, an element will continue reverberating for some short period of time, even though the elements facilitating it have stopped reverberating and stimulation from the environment has ceased.

An explicit rule for calculating the activities of the elements is necessary if this model is to be used in an actual simulation. For computational simplicity I suggest the rule:

OS4: Aside from the input elements, the activity of an element is the *sum of activity* passed to it by the reverberating elements of the attention span.

It is almost certain in fact that some other more complicated formula would reflect reality to a better degree. For example, if activity is transformed from cell assembly to cell assembly by a common subset of neurons, then two assemblies having some neurons in common might well pass activity to a third using only their common neurons, in which case there would be no simple summation of activity, but, instead, activity would be a rather complicated function taking this kind of interference into account. To some degree, the sloppy assumption made in OS4 is rescued by OS2 which allows only the most active elements to reverberate—any two functions used in OS4, however different the values they give for activity, will give the same effective results so long as they both arrange the elements in the same descending order from highest to lowest activity. And, with a computer simulation in mind, computational simplicity is at a premium. Where Hebb's original model depended only on the assemblies to direct activity, the inclusion here of the regulatory functions of the brain stem (as represented by OS2, OS5, and OS6) reduces the accuracy with which the individual activities need be calculated. Our only interest now is, which so-many elements are *most* active.

Human input and output structures are fantastically numerous and varied, but the nature of intelligence does not depend on their number, variety, or even on their exact nature. Beyond the specifications already given for the data structure, the way in which inputs generate activity from environmental conditions and the way in which outputs, by their activity, affect environmental conditions, are details of specific implementations (different for deaf or blind persons for example). The nature of intelligence does not seem to depend on these details (deaf, blind, and normal persons are all capable at times of intelligent behavior), so in a formalization of the functional invariants of intelligence, the details of input, output, and reflex link do not belong (except by way of example), so long as developability is assured (DS7).

The size of the attention span and the ease with which activity flows from one element to another are not constants of the system, but are varying from moment to moment. The reactivity of the nervous system must be constantly adjusted to meet the demands of the environment. If a sudden influx of signals from the environment is given to a highly reactive system (one with a high attention span and easy passage of activity from element to element) the total activity of the system may go too high and what we call confusion results— confusion that might not have developed if activity had not spread through the data structure so easily. In order to keep the system functioning with an optimum level of total activity, both the size of the attention span and the amount of activity passed along a link from a reverberating element might be varied. Such changes in reactivity are involved in the orienting and defense responses that have been observed and studied, behaviorally and physiologically, by Sokolov.

The orienting response is a change in reactivity that occurs when a novel stimulus is presented that does not pass activity to already functioning (reverberating) structures. The infant, gently stimulated, ceases motor activity and becomes alert and attentive. The orienting response has two distinct components. One is a decrease or cessation of ongoing motor (or more generally mental) activity, except for activity directly related to and supported by the novel stimulus, such as reflexive movements of sensory receptors towards the new stimulations. Formally, this is a decrease in the amount of activity passed along the links of reverberating elements. The other component of the orienting response is a generalized increase in the sensitivity to sensory inputs, and not only of the sensory receptors contacted by the novel stimulus, but by all receptors in all sensory modes. In the formal model, activity in an element is of little significance until it is high enough to place the element on attention. Since a change in the amount of activity flowing through links will change the activity of each element, but will not change the ordering of the elements by activity, it would appear that one way to get some of the less active elements into the attention span is to increase the size of the attention span so that it includes elements farther down the list in activity. Thus, sensitivity to sensory stimulation is increased. A novel stimulus will cause an increase in activity of elements not on attention, and, hence, a decrease in the proportion of total activity of all elements that is accounted for by the reverberating elements in the attention span. Therefore, the *central orienting response* will be formalized as:

OS5: Whenever the reverberation ratio (the sum of the activities of the reverberating elements divided by the sum of the activities of all the elements of the data structure) becomes smaller than a certain fraction, then the size of the attention span will increase at a certain rate until that fraction is reached, and the amount of activity passed along a link will decrease (in proportion to the increase in attention span?).

Once an orienting response has taken place, new elements on attention may (with sensory support from the novel stimulus) quickly come to control the motor outputs through reflex links. This is often seen as a part of the orienting response, but here we will view this as the natural consequence of the change in reactivity already formalized; the *central orienting response* is quite distinct from those very *local and specific orienting reflexes*.

What goes up, comes down and, indeed, the defense response is, in some respects, the opposite of the orienting response. In particular, a defense response involves specific and generalized increases in motor activity—a hand is withdrawn from pain at the same time a cry is uttered and the muscles throughout the body jerk convulsively. In any event, it would be formally embarassing if attention span could only rise and the activity transmitted by a link could only fall, so a formal inverse to the orientation response seems desirable and supported by the existence of the *central defense response:*

OS6: Whenever the reverberation ratio becomes larger than a certain fraction, then the size of the attention span will decrease at a certain rate until that fraction is reached, and the amount of activity passed along a link will increase (in proportion to the decrease in attention span?).

Just what the values of the certain fractions and rates in OS5 and OS6 are, and whether they have the same value for both OS5 and OS6 are relatively unimportant, just so long as control is maintained over the reactivity of the data structure. In modeling the brain as a part of the whole body system, the values in OS5 and OS6 may even depend on a variety of metabolic factors. Some justification for the formulation of OS5 and OS6 will be given later in Chapter 4.

As far as the internal data structure is concerned, reflexive circular reaction is a form of motor recognition because objects are recognized and treated differently only in terms of the different reflexes they excite. Each reflex, by nature of the many input and output elements (and links) that form a part of the reflex complex, may be excited by a number of different objects or events, and in this way the reflex generalizes to incorporate or assimilate in a circular reaction any object that stimulates its input elements. This is a form of *innate generalization*. The better feedback given in circular reaction, the more suitable an object is to the reacting reflex. Of course, different events will activate slightly different patterns of input and result in slight variations of reflexive motor output. The reflex is seen as accommodating itself to the given object.

The idea of exhaustion or weakening of the elements involved in a circular reaction seems to be unnecessary to an understanding of intelligence; when a reflex activity is dropped, it can usually be attributed to a loss of contact with the object, to competition from a new reflex pattern that becomes aroused, or by a general lowering of activities. The element itself is ready as ever to reverberate, but the rest of the system excludes it. For example, continued use of the sucking reflex may cause physical and metabolic changes which tend to pacify and put an infant to sleep, thus ending the sucking. In another case, the thumb may escape from the mouth and sucking may thus be ended. In general, the continued activity of a circular reaction (that is to say, the continued activity of the elements that form the internal part of a circular reaction) may change the environment and also the input configuration so that the support or stimulation of the ongoing activity by external events drops, while the support for other reactions increases (the muscles themselves may tire, sending back new sensations and requiring more stimulation to keep up their former tensions). In particular, pairs or whole systems of reflexes may, through kinesthetic sensations, operate together, and with no other external object than the body (opening and closing the empty hand, waving the arms, vacuous sucking and mouthing). The very stimulation caused by one motor activity which stretches certain muscles may be the input of an opposing reflex that tenses the stretched muscles.

At the very beginning, the reflexes seem obligatory, there is no conscious control over them and they apply themselves as the environment allows. The only driving force or motivation in this formal model is a tendency to incorporate or assimilate stimulations from objects into circular reaction. The usual concept of drive or motivation has been replaced by the concept of control and regulation of total activity at a certain optimal level. At the stage of mere reflex exercise, the infant is difficult to bore and may continue for what seem long periods in a single circular reaction. Also, the infant at this stage may appear to be transfixed by a pattern of stimulation (if he notices it at all); the infant may fall asleep watching a simple visual display. The usual neuron parameters of exhaustion or refractory period have, in this model, been completely submerged in the ideas of activity and reverberation. With continued stimulation, an individual element might reverberate endlessly without inter-ference from other elements or from the regulating system. Hebb specifically uses the assemblies to bridge the gap between the time scale of the individual neuron and of units of observable behavior, and where he insisted on the tiring of cell assemblies, it was only to account for phenomena that are explained here by the cognitive reflexes OS5 and OS6.

In summary, to explain the first stage of intellectual development, the stage of reflex exercise, we have developed a few general rules and specifications for an embyonic data structure and operating system. The purely reflex exercise stage lasts hardly a month for the human child, after which new developments begin to appear and predominate in behavior. Through subsequent stages we will follow the child's development and the basic formalism from this earliest stage will be refined, made more explicit, and enlarged, as required to understand the infant's developing behavior patterns. It turns out that very little more is required. For now, we have postulated a set of inputs, outputs, and reflexes. We know that they form circular reactions with the objects in the external world, the reflexes being said, in Piaget's system, to accommodate themselves to these objects and to assimilate these objects to themselves. The individual elements, which cannot remain active by themselves, thus can prolong their activity in a circular reaction with an external object. We have also postulated a system of functional rules that tend to regulate behavior by distributing activity from element to element. Activity passes through an element only if that element is reverberating, and an element reverberates only if it is among those elements receiving the largest amount of activity from the environment or other elements. The total amount of reverberation and activity is in turn regulated so as to maintain some sort of balance between incoming activity and outgoing activity.

Finally, some comment is needed on the lack of any rules of development for making changes or additions to the data structure. Changes take place in the data structure through use or experience; it is during this early reflex exercise that Hebb's first new assemblies are being formed. However, until they begin to intervene in the mechanical obedience of the reflexes to the environment, there is not much we can see of their effect on the system. Changes do take place during this first stage, but on a topologically restricted scale among the many elements (for example, sensory endings around the mouth) that actually constitute the one complex input element of the sucking reflex we have been considering here. An example of the earliest developmental changes is the learning within a few days to recognize the nipple on the breast. This sort of development within a complex is the same as the development we will later find taking place between complexes; only now, being more closely related in the first place, these changes take place much more quickly and locally. Largely because of the time sequence, Piaget (1936) classes such developments as Stage One behavior although they are really microscopic previews of later developments. Unfortunately, it is much more difficult to observe these earliest previews than it is to see the later developments simply because the present changes are not so dramatic and are only slight variations of basic reflex patterns—inborn and learned are at first difficult to distinguish. Simply noting that changes are occuring very early on a local scale, we move on to examine them in their more observable form between clearly separate reflex systems. After that, we will return to examine the more restricted changes occuring within a reflex complex.

Stage II: Primary Circular Reaction; Beginning in the Second Week

Behavior in the second stage, which extends roughly from age one to five months, is dominated by what Piaget calls the *primary circular reactions.* An example is the reaction between the sucking and grasping reflexes, whereby sucking an object may cause grasping movements of the empty hand, and grasping an object may lead to sucking behavior even though the mouth is not being stimulated. The primary circular reactions are distinguished from the reflexive circular reactions of the first stage in that the first stage reactions involve only one reflex (or perhaps several in succession) interacting in a closed loop with an outside object (or with the body itself), whereas the primary circular reactions of the second stage involve the simultaneous functioning of two (or more) reflexes. In what follows, a link is said to be functioning when the elements from and to which it points are simultaneously reverberating.

The first reflexive circular reactions were defined by the functioning of a reflex leading to the continued functioning of that same reflex as a result of an external event which tends to close the whole on itself in a feedback loop. Such a circular reaction needs no experience to operate; it results from an innate functional match between reflex link, input, output, and external event.

The primary circular reactions are defined by the functioning of one reflex leading to the functioning of another reflex, without external feedback. At first, a causative external event excites both reflexes which carry on reflexive circular reaction with the causative event. (An event might be the presence of the hand in contact with the mouth.) Later, the stimulation of one of these reflexes may also result in the motor outputs of the other reflex, even in the absence of the second reflex's usual sensory inputs. A primary circular reaction does not occur automatically; it requires that both reflexes have been used together in conjunction with the causative event and it represents a developmental change in the internal structure of the two reflexes—a change that did not occur passively, but as a result of the past functioning of the two reflexes.

The individual reflexive circular reactions involved in a primary circular reaction do not coalesce into a single unit. Each reflex is still capable of functioning independently of the other, although they now tend to facilitate each other. This results in a sort of reciprocal coordination between the two earlier structures; it is not an iron fast binding of the two. What sort of developmental change would this represent in the formal model: how might Hebb's (1949) assemblies relate to these changes?

The links of the formal model correspond roughly to the wired-in, diffuse, poorly differentiated neural pathways which conduct activity from one place to another within the nervous system. In Hebb's theory, some of these neural pathways pass through neurons in the cortex; there, groups of simultaneously active cells form into a cell assembly, and now begin to act as a single organized unit of the system. Created as it is from neurons on the pathways conducting activity from place to place, the new assembly comes ready made with links to and from other structures of the system. In the upper example of Fig. 2, two simultaneously functioning links (functioning in the sense that both their input and output elements are reverberating) will come to have an element or assembly through which they both pass, and which they are both capable of exciting to some extent. Activated (perhaps by just one of the links) and reverberating, this new element can then pass activity on to the two destinations of the original links. All this is added to, and does not replace, the original structures; the old reflexes may still be individually exercised. Hence, the developmental change in the data structure will be represented as the addition of the dotted element and links in Fig. 2. The formalization of this *developmental change* will be the following Data Structure specification:

DS8: When two (or more) links have been functioning at the same time (that is, the elements from which they point and to which they point have all been simultaneously reverberating) then, if not already done so, a new element is formed with links from the elements on the tail end of the said functioning links, and with links to the elements pointed to by the functioning links. The old elements and links remain. The new element is a *memory element.*

I will call the input and output elements primitive or *0th order elements,* and the new elements representing the first new assemblies will be the *1st order elements.* This way, a primary circular reaction is represented by a first order element coordinating two or more zeroth order input-output pairs. The primary circular reaction will involve the new coordinating element and perhaps all the elements of the old reflexive circular reactions it coordinates. In general I will loosely identify Piaget's schema and Hebb's cell assembly with an element of the formal model. Properly, an element of the formal model should only be identified as the smallest unit of schema, and some of Piaget's more complex schema and Hebb's cycles or phase sequences of cell assemblies should be thought of as a complex structure of elements.

Since an orienting response increases the attention span (OS5), it thereby increases the possibilities of learning and of developmental change. The more reverberating elements there are, the more likely is the creation of new elements on the links between reverberating elements. This is in line with the psychological evidence presented and interpreted by Sokolov (1963), Charlesworth (1969), and Berlyne (1960), to name but a few, from which it would appear that an orienting response does in fact greatly enhance learning, if it is not indeed necessary for learning. This significance of the orienting response has been included in the formal model as an interaction between OS5 and DS8. If a new element is created in a nonreverberating but active condition (perhaps inactive neurons are recruited into the structure of an assembly as it is built), then that new element may itself contribute to an orienting response since it will lower the fraction of total activity represented by reverberating elements. Thus, all learning would be accompanied by an orienting response.

Interpreting Piaget's terminology, we could say that the two reflexes coordinated by a first order element have changed or accommodated as a result of their mutual use or assimilation of an external event in circular reactions. *Assimilation* corresponds roughly to the passage of activity and accommodation corresponds to the structure of links and elements. Thus, we might say that a certain set of elements assimilates an object, or the sensory inputs from an object, when the inputs from the object result in increased activity or reverberation of that set of elements. Even more generally, when the links from one structure of elements

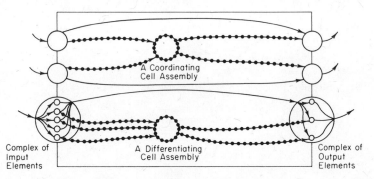

Fig. 2. The first cell assemblies are formed beginning stage two and primary circular reaction. At different levels of complexity the cell assembly appears to have two effects—coordination and differentiation. (The new structures are dotted.)

facilitate elements in a second structure, then the second structure assimilates or receives activity from the first. Thus, there is an active, *functional assimilation* in the actual functioning of a set of elements, and there is a passive *structural assimilation* implicit in the structure of a set of elements. Proceeding from assimilation to accommodation, we have discovered that functional assimilation may result in an accommodation of the assimilating structure: new links and elements may be added to the old structure. As a result of an accommodation, a structure may now be able to functionally assimilate new kinds of input, for example, the grasping reflex in the second stage is able to assimilate sensory inputs from the mouth. To complete the symmetry, there is an active and a passive form of accommodation. *Structural accommodation* is implicit in the new elements added to a structure, and *functional accommodation* is evidenced when reverberations pass from one part of a structure of elements to other parts, depending on the situation; the structure in effect accommodates its activity to the situation. Assimilation and accommodation are not separate processes, but, rather, different aspects of a single process; assimilation results in accommodation which in turn gives rise to new possibilities of assimilation.

Hand in hand with the development of new elements we find a change in the maximum number of simultaneously reverberating elements that may be expected. An increase in the total number of elements will (because OS5 and OS6 maintain a certain fraction of the active elements in attention) increase the average size of the attention span. Behavioral evidence for this may be observed. In early reflex behavior, we generally found that reverberations in one reflexive circular reaction tended to replace and halt reverberations in other circular reactions. With the developments of Stage Two, we may find two coordinated reflex patterns functioning simultaneously. For example, the infant engaged in nursing may now be observed to also engage in opening and closing the hand, even though there is nothing in the hand. Thus, the maximum number of simultaneously functioning elements seems to have increased. This may be a result of adding new elements to the system, or it may be that the addition of new elements to the system is a result of an increase of the number of elements allowed to reverberate at once. In reflex exercise of Stage One, we know that only two elements seem to function at once, one input and one output element. But for any new elements to be added, according to the rule of developmental change postulated above (DS8), we must have two reflex patterns simultaneously functioning, or at least four reverberating elements. One grand debate in psychology today centers around precisely this question: does experience and the addition of new elements increase the number of elements that may reverberate simultaneously (as implied by OS5, OS6, and DS8), or does some innate maturational process gradually increase the capacity of the brain to handle more and more simultaneously reverberating elements? There seems to be evidence pointing to both possibilities, so this developmental change should perhaps be stated separately as:

OS7: With time and increasing complexity of the data structure, the size of the attention span is increased.

It is of course tempting to relate the size of the attention span to Miller's (1956) famous value of 7±2 for the channel capacity of the brain as an information processing system. Attention span may, as suggested by Pascual-Leone (1970), mature from some base value to that base value plus Miller's; such maturation would (independent of experience) pace the development of intelligence through the stages outlined by Piaget.

We should take note of a very common developmental observation. As an infant matures, it is able to make finer and finer discriminations and its voluntary movements become more and more delicate and refined. With increasing age, it seems as if sensory patterns of less total activity are able to impress themselves on the consciousness and become incorporated into the memory of the child. At the same time, voluntary control gradually extends over the smaller movements which presumably also involve less total activity. During periods of attentive alertness, the child's arm flailing calms down to more gentle arm waving. However, if the child is crying or engaged in strong circular reaction such as sucking, this gentleness again disappears and the child's behavior looks much as it did previously; this refinement of discrimination and control is not only maturational, but, rather, varies with the child's degree of attentiveness to new stimuli, with his attention span. All this fits in with the system of reactivity control postulated in OS5, OS6, and OS7.

We might also note that OS2 stipulates that only the most active elements will reverberate so we might expect the infant at low attention span to be "conscious" only of those reflex activities that involve high activities in the sensory side. As attention span matures and more elements can be simultaneously reverberating, those reflexes with smaller activities are less likely to be crowded out; they can therefore become incorporated into memory by new coordinations. High activity reflexes, which are, presumably, crying, sucking, grasping, and the visual scan reflexes, will be the first to come under conscious control. Low activity reflexes such as eye blink, lens accommodation, and stretch reflexes of individual muscles will come under control only as the child matures. Very low activity reflexes, such as pupil constriction, vasodilatation, or piloerection, may never come under conscious control. Finally, we might recall that activity as used here means neural activity of a specific spacial and temporal pattern. Externally and behaviorally, such neural activity may be evidenced by motor inactivity as well as by motor activity. Not only can we activate a muscle, we can deliberately and selectively relax it. The effect of neural activity in some output elements may be to relax the muscles associated with it. Sleep and relaxation certainly involve strong patterns of neural activity as evidenced by the EEG. Transection of the spine does not produce relaxation, but, rather, intense muscular tension; the brain must constantly output a specific pattern of activity to relax the body. In fact, sleep is probably the highest activity reflex behavior of the nervous system, and the one an infant most often indulges in. Lumping sleep and strong motor activity together as low attention span, high activity per link behaviors may seem strange, but there is some justification. The infant, with a permanently depressed attention span, spends almost all his time sleeping or in rather strong (for him) motor activity.

We should now go back to examine the changes within a single reflexive circular reaction which we noted but ignored earlier. As an example, take the adjustment of the sucking reflex in its relation to the breast. As mentioned before, such a complex reflex actually involves thousands of sensory receptors in and around the mouth, and another large number of motor outputs and kinesthetic receptors in the muscles of the throat, lips, and neck (to mention a few). Each sensory input is, of course, not connected straight to a single motor output, but rather serves to excite the whole complex sucking response in some particular way. Perhaps each input should be represented as having links to several outputs. While the whole complex is engaged in reflexive circular reaction, different patterns of input elements are aroused by different objects. Each pattern then leads to the formation of a *perception* which is a cell assembly on the neural pathways from input to output aroused by that pattern of sensory stimulation. This cell assembly is a memory element that recognizes or assimilates the pattern of stimulation that led to its development. The result is a primitive recognition for the various objects that come in contact with the mouth. Some of these objects, and associated assemblies, are experienced in conjunction with more stimulating experiences than others. The nipple usually leads to a filling of the mouth with milk, and reflexive swallowing, when the sucking reflex is applied; this gives a stronger orienting response, a richer sensory input, and, hence, a greater variety of locations at which the cell assemblies can form. The nipple comes to be preferred by virtue of the greater number of cell assemblies it can arouse, and by virtue of the greater number of connections of each of these assemblies. These cell assemblies are connected to the larger number of inputs and outputs, and so may direct more movements of the head and mouth. Contact with the nipple thus has greater "meaning" or possibility of reverberation; it is more exciting to an inattentive baby (OS5), and more pacifying to an alert baby (OS6).

A more complex situation (but still classed by Piaget in Stage One), is the searching for the nipple on contact with the breast. This pattern of behavior will emerge as early as the second week, but never without previous experience. The seaching is directed in that the child can recognize the nipple, say on the left side of the mouth, and overriding stimulations on the right, orient the head toward the left. How can this be explained in the formal model? Perhaps this results from the insertion of first order elements that recognize (assimilate, receive activity from) the stimulations from the nipple. These elements would be formed on the pathways of the left orienting reflex between the touch receptors on the left side of the mouth to the muscles in the neck that move the head to the left. These elements would have been inserted because left head turning reflexes aroused when the nipple touched the left side of the mouth had in the past resulted in the relatively stimulating experience of the nipple moving into the rich sensory area of the mouth. A stimulating and rich sensory event is "rewarded" or reinforced by greater formation of assemblies than the sensually poor event where there was no nipple, but only a continuous surface of skin; no orienting response to new stimulations would have occured in the second case. Since assemblies form only on functioning links, the more reverberating elements and functioning links there are, the more new assemblies there might be. These new recognitory assemblies formed on the links of the left orienting reflex then facilitate a left movement any time thereafter when the nipple on the left stimulates these assemblies to reverberation. The stimulations from the parts of the breast on the right side of the mouth are ignored in favor of the more meaningful stimulations on the left, even though by themselves they may suffice to turn the head to the right. Here again, a more meaningful stimulation is one that is assimilated by more elements.

In similar fashion we might formulate the beginnings of the development of fixation in sight. Here the inputs are from the retina, and the outputs are the basic scanning movements of the eyes which are functioning at birth. In a manner analogous to the search for certain interesting objects near the mouth, the scanning reflexes would learn to direct the eye to an interesting, vaguely familiar, peripheral stimulus, in favor of a less assimilable stimulus. In another visual reflex system (and one that seems to mature only several weeks after birth) a fuzzy image without sharp edges might come to develop assemblies connecting it to the focusing reactions, accommodations of the lens, which had, in the past, resulted in the visually exciting appearance of a sharply defined image. At any time that scanning movements or lens accommodations are in progress, the appearance of an image near the fovea might result in an orienting response and consequent cessation of any motor activity in progress. Should the scan have overshot the visual image, then the image may result in yet another orienting response when the opposing scan (perhaps reflexively initiated by the kinesthetic feedback from the stretched eye muscles) again swings the image near the fovea. There may thus be an automatic reflexive circular reaction between two opposing scanning motions which would result in a narrowing of the scanning movements in the vicinity of an interesting visual image. Such visual activity is, in fact, reported by Salapatek for infants only a few days old. The creation of cell assemblies while narrowed visual scanning is taking place would then represent the earliest form of visual recognition and division of the visual field into recognizable subareas. Visual stimuli on the left become recognizably different from visual stimuli on the right. Once the scanning activity of the eyes can be fixed on a visual stimulus, recognitory assemblies could be formed by continued fixations of that visual stimulus.

Visual recognition would not, at this stage, be easily observed because there is little associated motor activity to indicate its development. However, in the case of the infant's own hand, the scanning reflexes will be able to track the movements of the hand, just as they might any other object. Recognitory assemblies will form, and in this case they will include in their structure links from concurrent kinesthetic inputs and links to concurrent motor outputs of the hand and arm. This results in a reciprocal coordination between hand and eye; anything looked at becomes something to reach for. Any visual excitation may, through innate generalization, suffice to activate the arm and bring a hand into the visual field. Then the eye-hand coordination can begin to function and direct the hand towards a visually interesting object. We might suppose that, in the past, the child has experienced the movement of the hand in conjunction with the visual image of the hand moving onto the fovea; cell assemblies would form and would be activated by a visual image of the hand in a certain portion of the visual field. These cell assemblies would in turn pass activity to those motor movements that brought the hand into full view. At first, the hand will only open and grasp when it touches or is very close to the target object, but at later stages of development, the hand may open in "preparation" for grasping, even as it is still approaching the object; the grasping reflex will in turn be coordinated to the visually directed reaching coordinations formed in Stage Two, or perhaps a larger, more mature attention span only later allows simultaneous reverberations in so many structures.

Those assemblies which are formed in a richer sensory input are the ones better developed; they have more links to other elements and so are functionally more likely to be aroused, and are structurally more likely to be developed. This could give a basis for the notion of reward; to a certain degree, increased sensory and motor activity is automatically "rewarded" by greater formation of assemblies. An examination of a particular case will amplify this notion. This is the case of the coordination of the arm flexion reflexes with the sucking reflexes.

In the first stage of sensorimotor development, the sucking reflex forms reflexive circular reactions with objects in the exterior world. In particular, the sucking reflex will use the infant's own hand to exercise itself, but, as Piaget observed, early in development the baby seems unable to keep the hand in the mouth. Given a hand immobilized by the infant lying on it, the sucking reflex will be applied if the mouth is in contact with the hand. But, unless held still, the hand escapes as a result of any movements of the body or any interference from the environment. The infant in the early stages does not know how to direct the hand back to the mouth, and can only suck on his hand as good fortune presents it. It is often the case that a more practiced and early maturing structure (the sucking reflex, visual scan reflexes) will be the first to try to exercise itself in a circular reaction with a given event (the hand touching the mouth, the hand in the visual field). Only later, the less practiced, later maturing structure (movements of the hands and arms) will try to exercise itself with the same event. Only when some of the elements of two structures are reverberating together will a new coordination between them be formed. Thus, at first, there is only the well-developed reflexive circular reaction of the sucking reflex with external objects in the mouth, and the two poorly developed reflexes (or coordinations—see the following discussion of differentiation of the reflexes) of the hand and arm which move the hand towards the mouth (arm flexion) and from the mouth (arm extension). If the arm flexion reflex is activated while the hand is in the mouth, the hand will be pressed to and remain in the mouth; the two structures may function some time together forming assemblies all the while. However, if the arm extension reflex is activated, contact of the mouth and hand will be broken, and the two will almost never be used simultaneously. Thus it is that arm flexion is rewarded in this particular context; it is the only reflex of the two that can operate in conjunction with the sucking reflex applied to the hand. It is the only one that can be reinforced by the formation of new assemblies on the simultaneously functioning links of the two reflexes. Finally, in the general anterior to posterior maturation of the embryo, fetus, and infant, the differential rates of maturation (DS6) may delay development of the hand sucking coordination until the maximal activities attainable by the arm moving reflexes are high enough to force their way to attention. In addition, attention span must be mature enough (OS7) to permit arm and sucking reflexes to reverberate together. Only then can the hand sucking coordination be learned. There may be a *critical period* when sucking and arm flexion are first able to function together; what happens during this critical period may profoundly affect later development.

Another development of the second stage is the *differentiation* of the basic reflexes into more specific activities, for example, the grasping reflex develops a scratching component, a stroking component, and eventually a whole set of *motor procedures,* each defined by a cell assembly. When the muscles have matured enough, the same thing will happen with the walking reflexes; they will differentiate under the influence of experience into running, jumping, dancing, and a variety of gaits. During any motor activity, there is sensory feedback in the form of messages from the sensory receptors in the skin and the position receptors or kinesthetic sense in the muscles. The various motions and positions of the body are constrained to a certain set of possibilities simply by virtue of the body's physical structure and by the available innate reflexes. Each reflex activity or position of a limb has a corresponding pattern of sensory inputs and concurrent motor outputs which, with experience, will lead to the formation of assemblies, or the insertion of new elements as a form of internal representation for these reflexes. This is shown in the lower part of Fig. 2. Thus, the reflexes are copied onto new areas of the cerebral cortex (or wherever the cell assemblies form). An example of a differentiated reflex is that of scratching at external objects. Scratching may develop as a coordination between certain sensations from the receptors around the finger nails, and certain motor activities of the fingers. At first, all motor activity of the hand may be a rather amorphous grasping reaction to any sensory input from the hand, but gradually the different kinds of inputs from the external world tend to capture and differentiate the particular muscular movements that produce them. Depending on the maturity of the muscles, all this may occur rather swiftly; a colt stands and walks within an hour of birth. Many instincts and reflexes are perhaps built into the logic of the body structure and not the brain. The nervous system only discovers and learns them.

As a further example of differentiated reflexes, it is likely that the flexion and extension of the arm are in fact learned in the second stage, or even the first. For each differentiated reflex the kinesthetic feedback passes through a cell assembly to the set of motor outputs that produce the differentiated response; past reflex activity of the set of outputs produced the sensory feedback which is now coordinated to the outputs. In this case the question that arises (and is not answered) is whether the coordination between hand and mouth is a second stage development or is some later development that coordinates a differentiated reflex of the arm which is itself a second stage addition. Such confusions of stage will be frequent, largely because Piaget has already made one classification, but the model developed here suggests another one based on hypothetical internal structures.

The arm motion which puts the hand into the mouth becomes rather specialized and automatic—quite distinct from the normal arm flexion. This motion may become yet another differentiated reflex on a par with the extension and flexion of the arm, but this learned "reflex," or procedure, as Piaget labels it, is coordinated and specialized to the sucking reflexes. This is but an example of a general phenomenon whereby the first order coordinations may interact with the reflexes to form still more first order coordinations; development leads to further development. Thus, the sucking reflex may interact with arm moving procedures to produce the hand-mouth coordination and, then, further specializations of the sucking and hand movements. In a similar fashion, once the hand-eye coordination is achieved, the visual image of the hand, in feedback through the eye, may lead to further differentiations of those hand movements that give particularly exciting visual images: wiggling the fingers, twisting the wrist. Through primary circular reaction, each reflex is brought under the influence of a whole new set of sensory patterns from the other coordinated reflex system. A new frontier of coordination and differentiation is opened up.

In the coordination of the auditory-vocal channels, the choking, swallowing, sucking, breathing, and crying reflexes all can produce noises and sensations in the throat which the infant can certainly hear and feel. As a consequence of simultaneous activity, the sensory patterns aroused by the production of sounds are connected by assemblies to the very motor activities that produced the sounds. Once this connection has been established, the infant may generate sounds purely for the sake of hearing them and exercising his auditory inputs, vocal tract outputs, and the recognitory assemblies between them. Some early examples are given by Piaget in Observations 1 and 2 of *Play, Dreams and Imitation in Childhood*. Within a few hours of birth, if a baby hears another baby crying, he may begin to cry himself, in a sense confusing the sounds of the other with the sounds he can produce himself. Perhaps, any noise will cause a newborn to cry; a later and clearer example is the infant's differentiation of the initial stages of crying, the brief whimperings that precede the full blown and prolonged wailing. Piaget presents a picture of the frustrated or angry baby who starts to cry, but on hearing the first few whimperings becomes interested in these sounds and begins to reproduce them. In terms of the formal model, the frustrated child might be one for whom a circular reaction has failed—the bottle has ceased giving milk. In such a situation, the sensory feedback giving activity to many elements begins to fall and a defense response sets in according to OS6; the attention span is reduced and activities go up—sucking becomes more vigorous. Finally, at a low enough attention span and high activity, only the most primitive and strongest respiratory reflexes can survive: those of crying or of sleeping (one or the other, depending on metabolic factors and facilitating kinesthetic feedback). Assuming that it is crying that commences, the initial auditory feedback may begin to activate cell assemblies that represent the differentiated reflex of whimpering. If there are enough of these assemblies, the increase in activity in nonreverberating elements may provoke an orienting response according to OS5, attention span stops falling or goes up, and the whimpering recognitory elements begin reverberation. Whimpering may then begin primary circular reaction and, through competition for a place on attention, whimpering may forestall or prevent the commencement of the more primitive reflex of wailing.

In general, Piaget points out that an infant at this stage will only imitate those sounds that he has already produced and, thereby, learned himself. This may occur simply through accident—in breathing, crying, or vacuous sucking the child may produce some noise which is immediately established by a new cell assembly as a differentiated reflex or procedure. However, once the child has thus learned to make a sound, he may reproduce it on hearing the same or an analogous sound produced by an adult. He cannot reproduce any others, and will not even try until later stages of development.

To summarize the important features of the second stage, the most obvious is the establishment of coordinations between what were originally independent reflexes. These coordinations are reciprocal, and this is represented in the model by a new element connecting the old elements of the primitive reflexes by links from the inputs and to the outputs of both primitive reflexes. The key abstraction from this stage is the particular way in which developmental changes are made. Thus, in hand-mouth coordination, at the same time that anything in the mouth may cause the hand to flex, anything in the hand may also cause the mouth to commence sucking motions. A bit later the arm movements are coordinated to the act of sucking, and anything grasped is promptly carried to the mouth and sucked, and anything in the mouth may cause the hand to move to the mouth. Finally, when the hand and eye are coordinated, anything looked at may be grasped, brought to the mouth, removed, and looked at again.

Another feature of the second stage is the *learned generalization* of a reflex by virtue of a coordination; generalization is implicit in the insertion of new elements. By whatever external event, object, or part of the body a coordination of two structures is first established, this coordination results in each of the more primitive structures becoming sensitive to the stimuli of the other. Again, the hand-eye and the hand-mouth coordinations illustrate generalization. Another example is the sound-sight coordination which may be caused by the frequent sight of the human face with its moving, noisy mouth. When a child begins to show interest in this moving face and watches it and makes noises at it, he is giving evidence of assemblies representing a sound-sight coordination (or perhaps representing a cerebral copy of differentiated primitive sound-sight reflexes). But the coordination is also innately generalized in that the infant may begin a search for visual stimulation in response to even nonhuman sounds with which he is not familiar. That the coordination is learned and not strictly an automatic reflexive one is evidenced by the fact that the infant actively searches from side to side until a human face is discovered. A simple reflexive search might be expected to direct the eyes only in the direction of the sound, and be terminated without preference for a particular visual pattern.

Yet another aspect of the insertion of new elements is that of differentiation. This is exemplified by the learned ability to reproduce certain sounds, having already (accidentally) discovered how to make them. A certain position or movement of the mouth and vocal tract is differentiated from other possibilities by the sound and other sensations so produced, and the sound is recognized and differentiated from other sounds by the same elements that coordinate and differentiate the movements of the mouth that may produce it. (Here is the epitome of sensorimotor perception.) Another example of differentiation is the development, through muscular kinetic senses, of motor procedures such as scratching, kicking, perhaps arm flexion and extension, and a whole host of basic motor skills. Even the primitive reflexes themselves may come to have cell assemblies representing them and thereby bringing them more into the realm of conscious, voluntary control. What was once automatic reflex becomes conscious choice dependent on which memory elements are reverberating. In general, reflexes may be differentiated by contacts with external objects (as when the mouth opens wide for some objects and not so wide for others), by interactions among themselves (as in hand-eye coordination when the infant learns certain movements of the hand and arm will bring it to the center of vision), by feedback through "public" channels (as in the case of learning to recognize and produce sounds broadcast through the air), and by feedback through "private" channels within the body (as in arm flexion, alternate opening and closing of the hand, arm waving, or sound production in the congenitally deaf).

Finally, the overall result of the insertion of new elements is that a greater number of opportunities and variations now exist for the exercise of the primitive reflexes. What is seen can now be grasped; all that can be grasped can now be mouthed and looked at. The various structures can begin to interact and cause further differentiation by exposing each structure to the stimuli of the others. Watching his hand, the infant may discover variations in its movement that he would otherwise have failed to notice or distinguish from kinesthetically similar movements.

Epistemologically, the cell assemblies reflect somehow the external realities. Thus, the elements coordinating hand and eye, or hand and mouth, are an internal representation of the hand. Once the hand has been thus internalized, its representation is further refined by new differentiations induced by the earliest coordinations (the hand-eye coordination induces later differentiations of visually interesting hand movements). Thus, the earliest coordinations and representations become the basis for the later ones. This might also form a basis for understanding social imprinting and attachment. Just as the hand is involved in many important early coordinations simply because it is the most mobile part of the human body and because, as part of the body, it is ever present for the nervous system to play with, so the mother is involved in many early coordinations (sight-sound, sight-of-mother and feeding, sight or sound of mother and physical activity or stimulation) because of her many varied activities and her frequent presence. Both hand and mother become learning focal points that many new behaviors relate to. The child begins to identify himself with (literally knows himself through the data structure which is a representation of) his hand and his mother. As new input and output elements mature, hand or mother is likely to interact with them before anything else and thereby cause the earliest (and perhaps therefore most important) coordinations and differentiations of the newly matured reflexes. Hand and mother are the most important things to imprint themselves on the developing data structure.

It will be convenient, in terms of the formal model, to define the second stage of development for any one reflex system as the insertion of new elements coordinating input and output of that reflex system to elements of other systems. (Such a definition of the second stage does not match Piaget's exactly, but does, I think, capture the spirit.) Once learning has begun and the second stage entered, there are two additional problems that must be solved by any formalization of learning. The first problem and the most important is the nature of the structure and organization of memory; DS8 gives a hint towards the solution of this problem. Another problem is the functional nature of memory, and an immediate solution to this problem is the assumption that it operates the same as the primitive input and output elements:

OS8: Memory elements are treated the same as the primitive input and output elements, except for those characteristics that refer explicitly to input or output elements (e.g., DS3, DS4).

This represents an *induction hypothesis* and, as stated, has gone beyond the functional nature of memory; it has also specified the developmental nature of memory. Memory elements are involved in development in the same way as input and output elements; specifically DS8 also applies to the memory elements. Memory develops out of memory just as it first developed out of sensorimotor structures. The first evidence to support this assertion will come in the third stage.

One last formalization should be made here. Is a unit of memory laid down gradually or all at once? (Once laid down, gradual or all at once does not matter; the ultimate functional and structural characteristics would be the same.) Even if a memory element is gradually built up, there must be something which remains between increments in its strength. (How can we increment something without something to increment to?) We might suppose this something is itself a memory element because it must be retrieved by the system to have its increment added. The only reason such a memory element might not be evidenced in behavior is that it may have so few links pointing to it that its activity is rarely high enough to reach reverberation—except at moments when the increments are added after an orienting response. How can increments be added? By coordinating the weak element to other elements, so that additional links facilitate the weak element and subsequent arousal becomes easier. Thus, an element might appear to build up either gradually, or immediately. If created from a large attention span, a new element may have many elements pointing to it and may be behaviorally functional after its initial creation. All this is implicit in the formal model as it now stands, and in a sense we can have it both ways. Hebb made a distinction between the slow rate of learning in early development and the fast, nearly instantaneous learning of later development. And Estes has since emphasized the concept of all-or-nothing, one-shot learning. To make it explicit:

DS9: Memory elements are created once and for all, though subsequently links to and from them may be added by DS8.

And, to make explicit the reverse process of forgetting:

DS10: Memory elements and links are not removed, though subsequent development may make it impossible to bring an element to reverberation.

The lost element may always be kept from reverberation by higher activity elements.

This ends the introduction of characteristics of the formal model; only elaborations remain. The model at this stage differs from the model in the final stages only in the complexity of its learned data structure. At this point, the newly formed coordinations are still directly dependent upon sensory input for their functioning. Intention or "will" as anything more than automatic reflex or reproduction of learned patterns is nonexistant. One could easily be misled into viewing the infant of four months as a rather complex input-output machine with memory; all the infant can do is give a specific set of outputs for a specific set of inputs, and add new paired input-output sets to his repertory if given them by his environment. Of course, everyone knows the infant escapes such automatism and achieves autonomy. Man can sometimes do more than slavishly copy and repeat; at his best, man can create and invent. Put as strongly as possible, I have hypothesized in the formal model that this is done by the anarchical use of a hierarchical structure. There is some developmental-structural device for recording as memory elements: not only input-output pairs, but also pairs of input-output pairs, pairs of these pairs, and so on, up to some order of elements (pairs) at least as high as three; and there is some functional device that can accept input and produce output by using all orders of elements indiscriminately and inter-mixed. (All this is but a startling way of describing OS8 of the formal model, and the three orders of abstraction we will discover takes us at least to the end, at age two years, of Piaget's sensorimotor period.) But, for now, can the child even escape his slavish discovery and reproduction of the input-output pairs given him by the environment? To do more than a mere translation from one pattern of inputs to some pattern of outputs, the coordinations of Stage Two must themselves come under the control of new structures, just as the primitive inputs and outputs have been put under the control of the coordinations.

Stage III: Secondary Circular Reactions; Beginning in the Fourth Month

In the second stage, coordinating elements were inserted on the links connecting input and output elements. These elements were the first internal representation of external events or objects and also of learned skills. For example, such an element is involved in both the perceptual image of the nipple (this image being patterns of sensory stimulation near the lips), and also the motor record that enhances motor response to the nipple. Sensory perceptions and motor procedures are the same things. Now, in the third stage, defined in this formal model as the insertion of yet another order of elements, there are *secondary circular reactions* between the earlier formed sensorimotor images.

Viewed from the output side, the structures of Stage Two become in Stage Three mobile procedures disassociated from any one particular input pattern and are applied to, or activated by, a variety of sensory input patterns, all by way of the new *second order elements*. This is exactly what happened in Stage Two when the reflexes were generalized to new inputs through coordination. Viewed from the input side, the structures of Stage Two become perceptions disassociated from any one particular output pattern and thereby become better representations of an object independent of its motor use. The new second order elements pass activity to, and are kept active by, their subordinate procedures and perceptions; secondary circular reaction involves two first order assemblies interacting through an external mediating event and an internal mediating coordination (the second order assembly).

At this stage, we can say a primitive form of intention exists in that the first order assemblies, or the procedures they define, are subordinated and driven by the second order assemblies to maintain an interesting event, to maintain contact with an object that arouses either of the subordinate assemblies. There can now be a coordination between a distinct memory element representing an elementary perception, and another distinct memory element representing a procedure—a means for rediscovering (or, perhaps, to the child, recreating) this perception. Although more generalized, the secondary circular reaction is still dependent on reverberations (high activities) passing from a sensory input element, perhaps through a first order element, to a second order element, and then down again through perhaps another first order element to an output element. There are more branch points along the way at which reverberation may pass to one of several assemblies, depending on which assembly is already best facilitated by yet other reverberating structures. Thus, a more variable, playful activity emerges in which the procedures exercise each other in circular reaction.

Let us trace the development of one of these secondary circular reactions. This will be the case of the swinging doll, leg shaking coordination in Observation 94 of *The Origins of Intelligence in Children*. In Stage Two development, before this observation was made, the child has formed a leg shaking procedure which is generally applied as a result of any pleasant excitement. In the model, this special skill would be formed as a coordination between the sensory patterns that result from leg shaking, and the motor output patterns that cause the leg shaking. A strong kick of the leg causes a general movement of the whole body in the crib and gives a global feedback from many parts of the body. Besides the leg shaking procedure, there is a doll recognition schema, or perception, involving the sight of some dolls hanging from the child's bassinet. Recognition is evidenced by a smile when the dolls are seen. (We will discuss the smile later.) The recognition of these dolls results from a coordination of the various visual inputs activated by the image of the dolls on the fovea; links from this perceptual element to the output elements of the scanning reflexes of the eye help the child to track the visual image of the dolls. The image of the doll gives general facilitation through its perceptual element to the tracking motions of the eye, and so may help maintain visual tracking procedures by facilitating their outputs. At some point, while shaking its legs, the child sees the dolls swinging, looks at them and begins leg shaking again. Within a day or so this becomes a definite reciprocal coordination. Chance swinging of the dolls causes leg shaking, and leg shaking from pleasant excitement causes the child to look for the dolls. The whole is spontaneously exercised by the child who lies shaking its legs and watching the swinging dolls. Functioning together, the old procedures are altered; leg shaking and visual tracking, as applied to the doll, become more systematic, sustained, and specialized. What kind of changes in the data structure are needed to explain these new developments? Just those postulated by DS8 and shown as the dotted structures in Fig. 3. In Fig. 3 (and in all the diagrams) the heavy lined elements are presumed to have been reverberating together and caused the formation of the dotted element. Reflex links are omitted for greater clarity.

This is the first time we have an element in which reverberation represents the functional selection of a pair of input-output pairs. Where the second stage coordination coupled together individual input and output elements into patterns of input and output, in the third stage the coordination couples together patterns of the patterns of the second stage. The induction hypothesis OS8 stands somewhat justified.

The new element and the structure of which it is a part is more generalized (or mobile, as Piaget says) than the previous structures because it can be aroused and used in an even greater variety of different situations. The new secondary circular reaction, as represented by the functioning of the entire structure in Fig. 3, serves to prolong and arouse the original primary circular reactions as a part of itself. Reverberation tends to remain longer in the secondary circular reaction which is aroused by more varied inputs and which contains a number of interfacilitating elements; overall activity of the system is more in the control of the larger structure, at the center of which is the new second order element. The element representing the new coordination is more mobile; it can remain active as other activities move between the two input or between the two output patterns. Each primary circular reaction can receive only one input and arouse only one output pattern.

Besides mobility and generality, the secondary circular reaction contains the beginning of intention. For Piaget, intention begins in the secondary reaction activating the primary reaction as a subsidiary activity for the functioning of the secondary reaction. One coordinated primary reaction may now be used to allow the functioning of the other, and both are subordinated to the continuing functioning of the greater whole. Also, anticipation and temporal sequencing

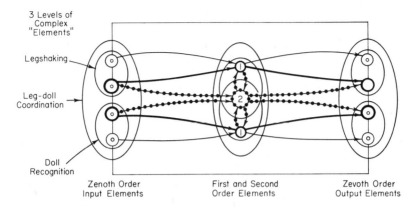

Fig. 3. New cell assemblies are derived from old to initiate the third stage and secondary circular reaction. (Reflex links have been omitted for greater clarity.) The new structures are dotted. Note: the order of a simple element is different from the level of complexity of a complex element.

begin here; leg shaking (used sometimes in order to start the already sighted dolls swinging) if aroused by other internal structures may, without visual sensory cues, also lead to visual searching for the anticipated swinging dolls. The secondary circular reaction represents a record of the chance discovery of an external connection between its component parts; it is also a record that can direct the rediscovery or reproduction or use of the external connection. The primary reactions serve to maintain and arouse the secondary reaction which, by virtue of its coordination of several primary reactions, can then continue its own activity with less dependence on any one input pattern. Although this independence is in no way complete (the secondary reaction really has only a larger, more varied input pattern, each piece of which was included explicitly by experience), the formation of the secondary circular reaction leads to more sustained and internally directed activity, perhaps seen by an external observer as evidence of will or intention.

Remember that each link of a complex element represents a number of roughly parallel links to only faintly different subelements of other complex elements. This is amplified in Fig. 3, where input and output are grouped in three levels of complexity. At the lowest level, the new dotted element is a coordination of some separate input and output elements. At the next level, the new element is a mixture of coordination and differentiation. Finally, at the highest level of complexity, with all input or all output elements enclosed by one circle, the new element is purely differentiation. When the new second order element and one of the old first order elements are both reverberating, the resultant output will be different from when only the first order element alone is reverberating. Similarly, from the input side, the secondary reaction has different sensitivities to input patterns from those of the primary reactions alone. The second order element introduces both coordination and differentiation, just as the first order element coordinated and differentiated the primitive reflexes; it gives more specific perceptions and procedures at the same time that it introduces mobility and generalization. The secondary circular reaction tends to break up subordinate structures into smaller, more specific structures at the same time that it coordinates the subordinate structures into a larger, more general one. Generalization and specific case reside in the same piece of coding.

The nature of differentiation would perhaps be clearest if each sensory and motor neuron was represented by an individual element in the model. Then the first order procedures would be clearly seen as a coordination of perhaps hundreds of roughly parallel reflex channels. (The scale of the attention span in the model would of course have to be changed; hundreds of small elements reverberating now replace a single large element reverberating.) Second order coordination would then involve only a certain subset (depending on the exact sensory and motor patterns of the coordinating event) of the input and output elements of the first order elements. The problem in building a specific model is one of deciding how finely to analyze behavior—how small an assembly of neurons is to be represented by an element. (I will side-step this issue and move freely up and down the scale, assuming the function and development to be pretty much the same. To do otherwise would require a book-keeping computer.) The confusion in Fig. 3 is only apparent, not real; only the lowest level elements need be considered.

A very important result of the secondary circular reaction is the creation of new differentiated primary circular reactions, not merely by its effect on the functioning of the old ones, but also by inducing the formation of yet another element. Again, coordination results in the opening of new frontiers. As an example, consider the discovery of a striking procedure described in Observation 103 of *The Origins of Intelligence in Children*. Lucienne has already developed the third stage hand-eye coordination, and while exercising it in reaching for a hanging doll, accidently strikes the doll rather hard, causing the doll to swing. Perhaps in failing to reach the doll, the lack of novel input to nonreverberating elements produced a "defensive" response as described by OS6; as a result of frustration, attention span goes down, activities go up, and the reaching is made stronger and more vigorous. In any event, the doll swings rather violently, causing first fear in the child (unexpected sensory input results in a strong, deactivating, orienting response), then pleasure and a smile (the new input arouses to reverberation some perceptual elements that assimilate the new input activities, a defense response ensues), and, finally, repetition (the original reaching structures were not forced off attention span by the orienting response but only lost enough activity to halt motor response; the defense response restores activities to a higher level, and the old motor actions recommence). A month or more later, the striking procedure is applied with increasing generality to other toys and is firmly established as a new primary circular reaction of the hand-eye secondary circular reaction that mediated its discovery through the sight of the violently swinging doll. The secondary reaction, because it facilitates both hand and sight structures simultaneously, greatly increased the chances that the striking procedure would be discovered through its visual effects, and incorporated immediately into an existing structure. The new procedure is represented by a first order element coordinating the input elements that caused the strike. The new procedure is also created with connections to the visual tracking and arm moving procedures, and with connections to the hand-eye coordinations. The situation is diagrammed in Fig. 4.

In Fig. 4, each element and link is meant to represent a complex with finer substructure. Each complex input element is actually a number of sensory receptors and closely related neurons that are capable of a number of simple firing patterns, and this is true of the other elements. Each complex link is meant to represent a number of parallel coordinations, all of them variations of arm movements; arm movements in different directions, of varying force, and for each arm. Also, the element representing visual tracking has a substructure of coordinations of the eye and neck muscles that track a visual stimulus and keep it near the fovea of the retina. The first order elements, in short, represent complexes of cerebrally copied and differentiated reflexes. And, finally, the second order element in Fig. 4 represents a number of secondary coordinations between some of the eye procedures and some of the arm moving procedures, for example a glance left, reach left, or a glance up, reach up coordination.

At the instant of the coordinating event (experience, lesson, or instruction), among the subelements of the arm moving complex there are some whose

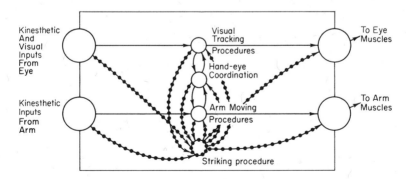

Fig. 4. Secondary circular reaction can induce new derived coordinations and speed the development of new structures. This kind of change is represented by the dotted structures.

current reverberations have resulted in a rather forceful sweep of the arm—a potential strike movement. But, if reverberating by themselves, they will only cause slightly different sensations in the hand and arm—sensations which they already assimilate, sensations which facilitate them anyhow. There is nothing else to distinguish this potential strike procedure from any other of the movements of the arm, they all coordinate inputs from the arm to outputs to the arm. However, since some of the arm moving procedures have already been coordinated to the visual tracking procedures, the child was watching his own reaching motions. Watching his own reaching motions, the child usually learns nothing new because, again, the coordinations have already been made. Piaget would call this pure functional and structural assimilation. However, when the hand accidentally strikes the dolls, the eyes receive, what is for this context, a radically new and unexpected sensation, one that sends activity into nonreverberating elements. The hand vigorously strikes the doll (unexpected sensation), and the doll swings violently (unexpected sensation). An orienting response is provoked and recognitory perceptual elements not already linked to the elements currently on attention begin reverberating; new coordinations are created between the now differentiated strike procedures, the visual tracking procedures, the newly aroused perceptual elements, and any other linked pairs of reverberating elements. All the possibilities are suggested by the dotted links in Fig. 4. The rapidity with which this striking procedure develops (it is immediately repeated over and over by the child as though the old structures had filled the attention span just to the optimal level, and now the newly coordinated structures just slightly overload the attention span and result in alternate orienting responses with attentive alert amusement, and defense responses with smiling repetition of motor actions) seems to imply that new, fully functional elements can be created by only one presentation of a new experience. The immediate repetition may only serve to exercise the new assembly, and, more microscopically analyzed, to create more substructure as further variation and elaboration of the newly discovered connection.

To quickly translate from this description to one of Piaget's, the arm moving schema has been made to accommodate and yield up a new striking schema or procedure which is created ready assimulated by all the old schemata. The new procedure itself assimilates the sensual experience and is subordinated to the old schemata in order to reproduce this interesting experience. Equilibrium, a process that keeps assimilation and accommodation in balance, has been the internal cause of all this. And, finally, this new schema is an accommodation that has resulted from playful activity or assimilation of new experiences by old schemata. But, in this case, the new experience was not quite assimilable, and the attempt at assimilation has resulted in accommodation.

The third stage represents the insertion of coordinating elements between the memory elements of the second stage. As another example, this may be what happens when the second stage procedures for left and right turning of the head become coordinated to result in deliberate and sustained head shaking, or the extend and flex arm procedures become coordinated into arm waving. This kind of back and forth reversability is a foundation for the spatial groups stressed by Piaget which are, at this stage, entirely subjective representations of body positions and movements.

We should take care to distinguish between reflexive alteration of opposing pairs of reflexes and deliberate, vigorous head, leg, and arm shaking. The developmental sequence might be as follows: in the first stage, the child reflexively turns his head to the left, and the stretch in opposing musculature evokes a reflexive turn to the right. In the second stage, cell assemblies are formed to give cortical representations for each of these individual movements which now become procedures; kinesthetic input while the head is turning one way facilitates the procedure for turning the head the other way. Finally, in the third stage, the two procedures are coordinated by a second order element which, when reverberating, arouses both procedures at once and results in a more rapid movement of the head with increased tension in both sets of opposing musculature. When the head shaking reaction can be seen to undergo variations in speed not explained by external events, we may suspect the third stage in the development of this structure to have been reached.

This interpretation of limb and head shaking presents certain problems for the earlier discussion of leg shaking in which the leg shaking was classified as a second stage procedure (following Piaget's own observational classification). The confusion is a natural one, and is easily understood by examination of Fig. 3. Here we can see that the topology of the second order and first order element is the same for both. The formation of the second order element changes the link structure of the first order element so the two are very similar. Both first and second order elements have links from input and output elements, and both now have links to and from memory elements (although, originally, the first order element has no such links). An even greater structural similarity is obtained if the first order element is now coordinated by yet another second order element to other first order elements. In such a case, an observer could hardly notice a difference in the characteristics of the second and third stages without knowing the precise developmental sequence. In the leg shaking, doll watching reaction described above, the leg shaking and doll watching eventually coordinated so that both could be carried on simultaneously. An observer could easily see that this is a secondary circular reaction because of the different sensory modalities and because leg shaking and doll watching clearly have learned components and must be at least second stage. But the leg shaking, by itself, is within one sensory modality, and how much of it is pure reflex and how much is learned, is unclear. If the stage of development is to be defined uniformly by the degree of complexity of the data structure, as done for the formal model, then we are stuck not being able to examine the data structure directly, and so must deduce and guess from incomplete behavioral evidence and history. In Fig. 4, we can see again how the second order elements and the first order elements are almost identical, their links are to and from the same sorts of elements. Only the history and the greater sensorimotor specificity of the first order or greater generality of the second order will serve to tell them apart.

As intimated earlier, we might also have to classify the coordination of the hand and eye in the third stage because it may actually consist of coordinations of what are in fact learned procedures, rather than coordinations between primitive reflexes. Stage, in part, depends on how microscopically we examine the structure, and how carefully we record the developmental history. If an observer considers the individual visual tracking and hand orienting movements as primitive unlearned reflexes, then he will classify the hand-eye coordination in Stage Two. But, an observer who considers each of these movements as being learned differentiations of a more primitive reflex would classify the hand-eye coordination in Stage Three. To decide between the two possibilities, we would need to know exactly what a child's innate reflexes are. Even without that we can still speak of stage as a relative thing; striking as described above is a Stage One development relative to the hand-eye coordination as a base structure.

Even when there are innate reflexes for each movement, the formation of cerebral copies through reflex exercise in the first stage will create procedures that can operate more independently of the inputs and contribute to stronger, more sustained reflex activity. These procedural copies of the reflexes may later exert greater control over the outputs than the actual reflexes themselves, but only after these procedures have been intercoordinated and so receive activity from more sources, do they become capable of higher summed activity than the individual inputs. The chief developmental significance of individual innate reflexes for each motor activity or highly specific localized orientation reflexes (not to be confused with the central, generalized orienting response), is that they give the child a head start in forming useful first assemblies which would probably be discovered only much later otherwise. And, in conjunction with the nature of the body, specific orientation reflexes help guarantee a continuing interaction between nervous system and environment (as stated in DS7).

A new phenomenon in Stage Three is the beginning of the *separation of sensory perception and motor procedure*. If only input elements and first order elements are reverberating (as when the infant stares fascinated at an object, or hears a familiar sound but does not respond immediately) then any new elements formed will have no direct links to output elements. Such differentiated elements are predominantly perceptual, but may easily pass activity through the original memory element to which they link, and then on to an output element. On the other side, if only first order elements and output elements are reverberating (the infant is vacuously practicing some of his motor procedures, perhaps with such weak sensory feedback that input elements cannot reach reverberation), then any new elements formed will have no direct links from input elements. Again, such elements are predominately procedural, but may receive input activity indirectly through memory elements. These possibilities are shown in Fig. 5. Unfortunately for the distinction made by the formal model between orders of elements, these new perceptions and procedures of the third stage have made the old first order elements of the second stage look much like a second order element itself. Here again are hints that the order of an element, and even the stage of development are becoming confused.

Once the secondary circular reactions are established, several things happen. The primary circular reactions proliferate and become more mobile and general; the events that once served to excite one of them may now excite others. The primary circular reactions are generalized reciprocally so that, in Lucienne's case, anything seen may cause leg shaking, and any leg shaking may cause a search for something to see. This is exactly the same as in Stage Two where anything sucked became something to grasp, and vice versa. In another respect, Stage Three resembles Stage Two. This is the increase in variability of behavior. Any one behavior pattern may now seem to die away of its own accord instead of applying itself until external conditions terminate it. For example, instead of prolonged sucking of the thumb, the child may now spontaneously stop sucking the thumb to take it out of the mouth and look at it, perhaps as a result of coordinations between sight and kinesthetic sensations of the hand being near or touching the face. Or the child might now give up leg shaking and spontaneously begin a search for swinging objects on its bassinet. Thus, there are longer internal transfers of activity mediated by the second order elements, and as reverberation passes from memory element to memory element,

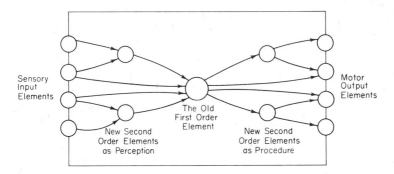

Fig. 5. The separation of perception and procedure.

there is the beginning of Hebb's phase sequence, a train of thought, and of Piaget's anticipation, intention, or will.

At the same time that we, as external observers, might begin to attribute will or intention to the child, the child might begin to attribute "will" and "intention" to the things in his environment (us in particular). From our egotistic point of view, we might say the child is becoming aware of objective reality; the first form of object permanence appears. When the stimulations that are activating a procedure disappear, another related procedure may be activated through secondary circular reaction which reestablishes contact with the lost object on another set of sensory inputs. Even without direct sensory contact, the child "knew" it would be there. Only by involvement in two or more independent internal structures is the objective existence of something in the environment recognized and elaborated. Otherwise the object is only an adjunct to the functioning of an old structure. But when the child activates one structure and finds the other structure aroused independently of his own intention or control (i.e., internal data structure), he becomes dimly aware of an existence, an external will independent of his own.

As more and more secondary circular reactions are established, each using perhaps the sight of a doll as one of its coordinated components, they tend to compete with each other; they are all aroused about equally well by the sight of the doll, but the limitation on attention span allows only the ones with highest activities to reverberate. Eventually, the sight of the doll may only elicit a very weak leg shake before another structure crowds into attention. In the end there may be only an internal recognition in the form of the brief activity of memory elements without actual motor response.

The third stage has been a continuation of the data structure's development, and it has not been necessary to make changes or addition to the operating system of Stage Two. However, with greater complexity of structure, we can see more clearly the selective retrieval properties of the operating system's functioning. When several procedures are being activated, the operating system retrieves or selects only the most active, most relevant ones for reverberation. This might be evidenced when the child stops shaking its legs to look for the swinging dolls, and resumes shaking when the dolls stop swinging. The procedures most stimulated by recent events are the procedures actually used. When the dolls are swinging, visual tracking is the most stimulated procedure; when the dolls stop swinging, leg shaking becomes relatively more likely. And, given that the dolls are out of reach, seeing them arouses the leg shaking and not the attempts to grasp, although the child will reach and grasp when the visual image of the dolls changes in a certain manner as they come closer. This selection of the most aroused or appropriate procedure is not a new phenomenon; it was involved when the child oriented his mouth to the side that sensed the nipple. But with the elaboration of competing procedures, we can more easily see behavioral evidence for the factor of attention. This factor was of course stated in OS2.

In the nervous system, the limited number of elements that may reverberate seems to be determined in part by the reticular activating system in the brain stem which is sometimes viewed as monitoring the overall activity of the nervous system and regulating, accordingly, the reactivity of the cerebral cortex. A neurological interpretation of the model would have to refine the statement of OS2 to match the quantitative properties of the reticular activating system and brain stem. A computer interpretation would refine OS2 only to ensure that enough elements were active to allow swift learning and efficient functioning. In any case, the practical effect of this self-regulation is the following: if the elements of the system are relatively inactive, a controlled number of elements, even though low in activity, will always be made to reverberate—slight increase of input will attract attention. If the system is relatively over-active, still only a controlled number of elements will be allowed to reverberate; this tends to hold activity down. Without this kind of central regulation, when total activity is too great, then even irrelevant assemblies may have high activity and push their way to the top; confusion, insensitivity, and spasmodic motor outbursts may occur. When total activity is too low, important assemblies may fail to reverberate and familiar sensations will not be properly interpreted, or old skills may not be performed smoothly or correctly.

The statement of OS2 which postulates a central control seems superior to a threshold formulation where each element has its own threshold; the amount of activity required to start an element reverberating may vary depending on the rest of the system. When there is little total activity, it takes less to arouse any one element to reverberation, but when the level of activity rises, all the lowest threshold elements do not begin to reverberate. With a threshold for each element, there must also be some sort of inhibition specifically built into each element to produce a dynamic balance of reactivity, later additions to the data structure may upset this balance. With a central, data-structure-independent inhibition, rather than having complicated plus and minus activations for each element that must nearly balance out, the thresholds of all elements are in effect varied from moment to moment to maintain the desired level of activity; the details of the data structure are greatly reduced in the model, and this is most important if we have computer simulation in mind. In addition, the formulation of OS2 provides not only for central control of functional reactivity, but also of developmental change; only the most relevant links are used to form new elements, as in the differentiation of the striking procedure. And, through the regulations of attention span by OS5 and OS6, the rate of learning is varied so that it increases precisely at those moments when something new and unexpected occurs.

Finally, strict account must be made of the use of the word "pleasant" in describing above the leg shaking schema. We usually suppose that pleasure is involved in an activity if that activity is accompanied by a smile. This child is pleased to recognize familiar toys and sensations, or finds pleasure in bouncing himself by shaking the legs—that's what we say. But, what we see is a smile. Where did the smile come from? What are its structural, functional, and developmental characteristics? Wolff has traced the smile back to the first week of infancy where it originates in a sort of facial grimace that occurs, at first, only during irregular sleep or drowsiness, and particularly just as the eyes close. This earliest smile seems to be a reflex which is best aroused at low attention span and high neural activity. In particular, it may be that this early smile is a part of the general defense reflex described by OS6; the smile often occurs spontaneously just as the infant is falling into a state of sleep. The adult grimace from pain or exertion may be another development (or rather nondevelopment) of this primordial defensive smile. In the first week of life, when this early smile is elicited by stimulation, it has a very constant and long latency period—6 to 8 seconds. How might this grimace of defense become the smile of recognition and pleasure?

Stimulation should produce a general orienting response as described in OS5, and if the stimulation is short lived, the orienting response might be followed shortly by a rebound defense response and smile when the changed state of the body (itself a result of the orienting response) produces enough kinesthetic feedback to cause reverberations. This would account for the long latency of the early grimace—it is no simple reflex, but a reflex that involves two changes in the reactivity of the whole nervous system and body with consequently longer time constants. A few weeks after birth, when the smile appears during wakefulness, it is different morphologically—it is more generalized, and involves more muscles of the whole face (as a consequence of larger attention span and more elements). It is best elicited now by the human voice—a familiar stimulation (which provokes an initial orienting response, followed by a prompt defense response as recognitory elements reach reverberation) and its latency goes down to about four seconds, or even two (because of the prompt recognitory reverberations). At this point, the future course of the smile's development comes under a profound influence. It turns out that the smile is an effective mode of circular reaction with something in the environment—the parents.

Recognition produces a smile or grimace, is pleasant, and would be evidenced internally by an initial orienting response to a new stimulation, then a sudden increase in reverberation, and finally a consequent defensive lowering in the attention span. Following Hebb's lead, we might therefore identify as pleasurable those experiences that move the attention span back towards the optimal level of total reverberation. Stimulation or thought that makes the attention span too large (excess inescapable, unfamiliar stimulation and anxiety) or too low (pain, excess reverberation from even familiar stimulation, depression, boredom with an overlearned and too strongly self-facilitating structure) is unpleasurable. Of course it is always possible that metabolic changes may alter the optimal level of attention maintained by OS5 and OS6, so that states of sleep and alertness may alternate.

In Stage Three, the fortuitous discovery of an external relationship has led to the formation of a new second order of elements and of new procedures to maintain them. In the next stage, the functioning of these second order elements leads to the discovery, by intuition, of a new external relationship.

Stage IV: Familiar Procedures in New Situations; Beginning in the Eighth Month

Piaget's fourth stage is a natural consequence of the second order elements created in Stage Three. However, a very significant change in the functional behavior takes place. For the first time we observe the application of known schemata or procedures in new situations, with environmental events quite different from the ones that led to the creation of the schemata. This is diagrammed in Fig. 6 which shows a *chain* of interlinked elements.

The element labeled X in Fig. 6 is a second order element between two first order elements. The creation of X was caused by some event in the past, and X represents the memory of that event. A different event caused the formation of the other second order element Y which happens by chance to have one procedure in common with X. The fourth stage is reached when one of the procedures A, B, or C is applied in a situation which it does not immediately assimilate. Suppose, for example, that some environmental circumstances have caused the reverberation of the input elements to A, B, and their coordination, X. Then, in normal secondary circular reaction, the procedures A and B are exercised. This is simply a reproduction or acting out of the coordination or memory represented by X, and is typical of Stage Three behavior. But, if A cannot proceed (for example if A is a reaching procedure and the object is too far away), there is surprise at the unexpected result; sensory feedback fails to maintain reverberations in A or in some anticipated perception, and an orienting response is evoked. Attention span is increased and new elements are admitted to reverberation while the motor activity of procedure A is stopped. The failure that caused persistent reaching in Stage Three (Observation 103) now causes an orienting response because the more complex system now anticipates and senses failure as novelty. Element A is aroused by X, but this anticipation is not confined by direct sensory input. Now, after the orienting response produced by failure of A, the element Y may begin to reverberate and pass activity on to the procedure C. If C is appropriate, that is if it already has some activity (but formerly not enough to reverberate), then the extra activity from Y may finally initiate reverberations in the procedure C. If coordination Y, indeed, begins circular reaction, then this represents an application of a familiar procedure, C, in a new situation—the situation that normally arouses A and B. It is possible that the child has never before experienced A and C together, but only A with B, and B with C, so that this is the first primitive form of invention.

In the most dramatic case, the application of C will change (accidently) the situation so that the original procedure A may become appropriate and be successfully applied; the child has discovered, by a very brief chain of thought, a means to an end. This discovery is promptly recorded; the near simultaneous reverberations of C, and then of the inputs of A and of A itself, will cause the formation of a new element which now coordinates A and C directly. A form of shortcircuiting takes place.

The new element created in the fourth stage is formed in a slightly more memory dominated data structure than were the elements formed before. The proportion of memory elements (in contrast to the input and output elements) that are reverberating when the new fourth stage element is created, is going up. When the first order elements were created, there were no other memory elements involved, only input and output elements. When the second order elements were created, the first order memory elements represented a third to a half of the reverberating elements from which the new element was formed. Now, in the fourth stage, the memory elements constitute nearly a half, and up, of the reverberating elements from which new elements are formed. And, since memory elements may interfacilitate each other in completely internalized closed loops of elements and links, the possibility is arising that some memory elements may be created with no direct links to input or output at all. But this comes later.

In Fig. 6, the more closely C is related to the original input that aroused A and B, the more easily C will be aroused rather than some other procedures. Thus, a set of related procedures are coordinated together fairly quickly by second order elements so that any one procedure is connected to all those other procedures which in the past have aided its own functioning. It may even be the case that what prevented the application of A was an obstacle with its own set of input stimulations which helped to arouse C. These inputs from the obstacle are then included in the new secondary circular reaction set up between A and C, so that in the future the presence of this obstacle may lead directly to the application of C, and then of A.

The coordinations of Stage Four have only been confirmed by the environment but have been invented, suggested, and discovered in memory by

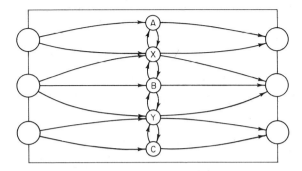

Fig. 6. The structural requirements for the application of familiar procedures in new situations; a chain of memory elements.

the child himself. The coordinations are not imposed by the present circumstances, indeed, they may not apply at all; C may have nothing to do with A. Still, because there is sense to the world, similarity, transitivity, and analogy often work. Therefore, this capacity for trying old procedures in new situations will now greatly speed the child's development and guide his activity in a direction that is increasingly often rewarding. All the processes of differentiation, perceptual and procedural growth, and coordination which we saw in the third stage will continue at an increasing rate.

Novel as fourth stage behavior appears to be, it is implicit in the second order elements of the third stage, and only awaits the addition of enough second order elements before the first inventive jump is possible along two accidentally intersecting secondary circular reactions. It seems strange that this does not occur for so long after the beginning of Stage Three. There are at least two reasons for this. The first is a problem already encountered, that of classifying behavior into stages and of knowing how finely to analyze it. Without knowing the developmental history of some pattern of behavior, it is impossible to decide what stage it is entering. And often small localized changes within a single behavior pattern are overlooked, even though they may be entering higher stages of development much earlier than the more dramatic changes that occur between clearly separate patterns of behavior. What Piaget classified as the first stage of the sucking reflex, on close examination is structurally identical to the later coordinations between hand and mouth. Therefore, we might presume that fourth stage changes as defined in the formal model are occurring on a local scale that is easily overlooked or included as variations and substages of the third stage.

A second reason for the delay in the onset of the fourth stage may be maturational factors. In particular, fourth stage behavior may depend on having a certain minimum of attention span which might not be reached until about the age of nine months. Only after a certain complexity has been reached by the data structure might the fraction of total activity maintained in attention span by OS5 and OS6 be such as to allow enough elements onto attention span to commence with Stage Four developments. Thus, as the number of elements and their links increases, the activity that can leak out of attention span to nonreverberating elements also increases, and thereby the size of the attention span increases. This is because OS5 and OS6 maintain a fixed fraction of total activity in the attention span which must therefore increase as the total activity in the data structure increases due to the development of memory elements. Another possibility is that the attention span matures biologically and independently of the accumulation of experience. (According to the natural principle of maximal confusion, both possibilities must surely be the case.)

Why fourth stage behavior depends on a sufficiently large attention span should be clear. Reverberations must span the distance from the procedure that is first applied to the procedure that is next applied. In the example given in Fig. 6, there must be reverberations in the common procedure B, in the coordination Y, in the procedure C, and in the outputs of the procedure C, at least. There are other combinations of reverberations that may finally result in the circular reaction of C, but they all require a larger attention span than the simple requirements for the earlier stages, especially Stages One and Two.

With the increasing number of chained secondary circular reactions, the mobility of the procedures increases, and more and more derived secondary circular reactions, such as that between A and C, are generated. Also, the increased number of secondary reactions leads to even more primary reactions, just as in Stage Three. In general, the developmental trends of Stage Four are but continuations of those of Stage Three. The typical behavior of a child in Stage Four when given an object appears to be exploratory; one after another of the chained procedures are applied to the object.

A clear example of Stage Four behavior is the removal of an obstacle as detailed in Observation 122 of *The Origins of Intelligence in Children.* An object is placed in sight of Laurent, but an obstacle is also arranged so that the child cannot grasp the object. A series of observations are made ranging over a period of a month. Each time, Laurent has a number of procedures and coordinations which he applies. He begins by locking his visual system on the object; the visual tracking procedures act here as the central procedure (B in Fig. 6) from which other procedures may be activated through secondary circular reaction. He attempts to reach directly for the object (procedure A), but failing because of the obstacle, applies a series of procedures already coordinated to the visual tracking initially aroused. He tries to move around the obstacle and fails. He waves his hands, shakes his head, his legs, and generally applies whatever procedures occur to him. Finally, one day, he strikes out and hits the obstacle, removing it. When reaching is subsequently tried, it succeeds. In later observations, upon failure of the reaching procedure, Laurent promptly applies the striking procedure to the obstacle and grasps the object. The reliable and prompt reproduction of this behavior, in contrast to the groping observed at first, is evidence that a coordination has been formed between reaching and striking. The coordinating element may even be facilitated by perceptual or input elements which recognize an obstacle as any sizable object between the child and the goal. In reaching for a goal, the obstacle is encountered, visually or by touch, and the striking procedure is aroused.

It is very interesting that the child is able to apply his newly learned striking-in-order-to-reach coordination in a variety of circumstances. The goal, the obstacle, the exact movements required to strike the obstacle, may be quite different in each case. Still the child is able to aim his blow, and to generate his new skill to a potentially endless variety of situations. This is the phenomenon of motor (and sensory) equivalence. Various sensory patterns are used equivalently by the new coordination—even though they have never been experienced with the new coordination before. Various motor activities are used equivalently for the same end. The striking procedure has brought with it a whole complement of perceptions and subsidiary procedures that were built up during the third stage. These are the second order elements diagrammed in Fig. 5. Now, the coordination of the fourth stage between striking and reaching is formed with all these substructures automatically included. This is the significance of recording in memory not merely paired input-output patterns but also pairs of input-output pairs, and pairs of pairs, and so on. The new higher order accommodations are created ready for immediate generalization.

Another example of fourth stage chaining behavior, described by Bruner in *Studies of Cognitive Development*, occurs on a more local scale and at an earlier age. This is the case of the reaching-to-grasp reaction which begins with three chained procedures: the visual tracking procedures (represented by B in Fig. 6), the arm extension procedures (represented by A), and the grasping reflex (a differentiated cerebral copy of which is represented by C). There is also the hand-eye coordination or secondary circular reaction (represented by X), but that is all (there is no Y coordination). What happens is this: the very sight of an interesting object is enough to bring the hand into the visual field and guide it towards the object; this is mediated by the hand-eye coordination X. Then, on contact with the object, direct sensory feedback from the hand arouses the grasping procedures, C. This close association of seeing the hand near the object and of feeling the object touch the hand may lead to the formation of a coordination between visual and grasping procedures. Thereafter, the hand may open for grasping when it is visually near the object to be grasped. Finally, we find that the hand opens even before it is near the desired object. Thus, either the reach and grasp have become linked by a fourth stage coordination, or the attention span has grown so that the simultaneous activity of all three procedures is possible.

Fourth stage coordinations may be quickly elaborated as the implications of the lower structures which they coordinated are worked out. In the case of the striking-to-reach coordination discussed before, striking is not necessarily the best procedure to use; it was merely the first successful one discovered. The most useful procedure would be simply pushing the obstacle aside, and, indeed, in subsequent practice, the child discovers this. In the motor equivalence set of the striking procedure (that is, in the set of subordinate procedures as diagrammed in Fig. 5) there are various motor movements of varying degrees of intensity and in various directions. These subordinate procedures are what allow the immediate generalization of the striking-to-reach coordination to new situations. In exercising his striking-to-reach coordination in new situations, the child will vary his use of the subordinate procedures to meet each situation; each new situation arouses different subordinate procedures. Gradually, and only as chance experiences dictate, the child learns which subordinate procedures are most useful; some of the subordinate procedures are themselves coordinated directly to the reaching procedure, and further differentiated by increased use. (Later, in the fifth stage, this process of elaboration will be carried out immediately upon discovery of a new coordination, rather than as dictated by subsequent chance exercise. The child will appear to be interested in the procedures themselves rather than in their immediate effects and usefulness to him.)

As a further example of the fourth stage, consider the following from Observation 130. Laurent has just learned to let an object fall, not to see it fall, or hear it drop, but, rather, apparently just feeling the sensation of it slipping from his fingers. Also, an earlier coordination has been observed a month ago in which the child strikes a metal basin with an object held in the hand, apparently to hear the noise produced. Laurent is playing at dropping an object (learned only the day before), when a nearby metal basin is struck by the experimenter. The child grasps the object he has been dropping, holds it over the basin, and lets it drop, thereby reproducing the noise. The basin is moved, but the child still succeeds in dropping the object into the basin. In this situation, the grasping procedure is a subordinate procedure of two different coordinations, the striking-to-produce-noise and the grasping-to-let-fall coordinations. One of these coordinations is being exercised when the sights and sounds of the other intrude. Through the common grasping procedure, the grasping-to-let-fall coordination is activated as a means for producing the perceptions of the striking-to-produce-noise coordination. In a sense, the old structures are decomposed and recombined to produce a new behavior; reverberations spread from one structure to parts of the other, through common elements and through facilitation from the environment. And there is immediate generalization in that the child can aim his drop as the location of the basin is varied. This is implicit in the subordinate procedures and perceptions of the old structures.

A few possible confusions should perhaps be cleared up here. Generalization of a behavior may take two forms. Innate generalization is simply a forced assimilation of any suitable object whose individualities are ignored. Thus, almost anything can be grasped. A more complicated learned generalization is implicit in motor and sensory equivalence. Here the individualities are attended to and accommodated, and appropriate substructures are used. Thus, in reaching for almost any object to grasp, aim must be made, and the hand must be opened more or less widely to fit the object. A second confusion may be that at one time grasping is a procedure, at another it is a subordinate procedure, and at still another it is a perception. This is not a confusion on the part of the observer (or the interpreter, or the reader); this is a reflection of a genuine strength of the operating system. Once an element has gotten attention it is treated no differently from any other element, whatever its "order" or its connections to other elements. Like all the others it simply begins passing activity down its links. Depending on which of its facilitated elements manage to come to reverberation, the element may have different behavioral results, one time seeming only a perception, another time seeming to be a procedure with motor results. Thus, all the petty distinctions we are wont to make are likely to be violated in fact. Perception, procedure, and coordination are all matters of degree and of context. Though they help us to think, in fact, the central processer, by ignoring them, gains great flexibility in decomposing old structures (by selecting only certain parts for attention), and in recomposing these into new structures.

In this stage what Piaget calls the sign first appears. The sign is a set of sensory inputs which would normally arouse a particular procedure or perception. But, with the insertion of secondary circular reactions, this pattern of input activity becomes a sign to the other procedures it can arouse through the secondary circular reaction. These other procedures are perhaps quite removed from, and independent of those directly linked to the inputs representing the sign; chains of links and coordinations may transform the reverberations of a sign some distance. As an example, in Observation 133, Jacqueline knows by the sound of the spoon on a glass or bowl that the spoon came from a glass of juice or a bowl of soup. Without even looking at the spoon, she knows what will be in it and opens or closes her mouth accordingly. The sound of the spoon on a glass does not normally cause the mouth to open. It is because of the very recent discovery that different sounds are associated with different tastes, that the sound of the glass is coordinated with the perception of a pleasant taste, and it is this coordination that opens the mouth, in anticipation of the mouth watering flavor of the juice. On the other hand, the unpleasant soup may in the past have been spit out, so the soup's perceptions actually facilitate expulsion and closing of the mouth. When the sign arrives from the bowl, the reaction is a clamping of the mouth. It may be simpler to assume direct associative links between the sounds and the motor activities they produce, but then the source of our introspectively discovered anticipations of perceptions is left out. The chains of coordinations and procedures lead to an elementary form of prevision. Using again the diagram in Fig. 6, the sound of the spoon on the glass may be represented by the element A (which is now a "perception" linking a certain auditory input to head orienting movements), and the activity of mouthing the juice may be represented by the element B which is now a perception of certain tastes and facilitates a procedure, C, that opens the mouth.

Another example of prevision is given in Observation 133. The sight of a bottle of alcohol produces crying from Jacqueline whose usual reaction might be to reach for bottles, but who has only once had a scratch treated with the alcohol. Here the perception of the alcohol bottle has in the past been coordinated with the perception of the accompanying pain and the resultant crying. It is interesting that this coordination took but one experience to form, and still it is particularly strong, overpowering all other possibilities of reaction. At this stage, the child's attention span has matured somewhat and therefore the number of reverberating elements that may contribute to the formation of a new coordination is larger. At this age, the single experience with the alcohol bottle may cause the formation of a coordination that has a considerable number of links facilitating it. Even though exercised only once, this coordination may be aroused to relatively high activity by rather specific kinds of situations, those situations that cause reverberation in exactly the same elements that were reverberating when the new coordination was formed. Thus, as attention span matures, new elements become more easily aroused by more specific situations; even without intervening exercise, a memory may remain retrievable. And without the intervening exercise and associated differentiations and elaborations, a memory may remain relatively specific.

Although it is possible that the mere association of the alcohol bottle and the pain and crying may account for later crying on presentation of the alcohol bottle alone, there always seems to be something real about crying that simple association does not explain. If we assume that crying is a defense reflex, or, more particularly, that it is a high activity, low attention span reflex like sleep, then a functional explanation of the fear of the alcohol bottle, is possible. In general, crying may result from any excessive stimulation, and particularly from excessive stimulation that is not familiar or assimilable and with which the child cannot begin a circular reaction. Such stimulation might bring a few elements to reverberation with high activity, but, being strange, pass little activity on to nonreverberating elements. Under these conditions we might expect a defensive lowering of the attention span in the formal model, and observationally we know the child is likely to cry. In the case of the alcohol bottle, the sensory input is certainly familiar, but the specific memory element is poorly linked to any activity but that of crying. Thus, not only might the recognition of the alcohol bottle facilitate crying, but also its very familiarity may have evoked a strong orienting response just prior to recognition. Jacqueline is transfixed by fear. Then, with recognition, an unusually strong defense response may be evoked because the elements that are reverberating pass so little activity on to nonreverberating procedures and coordinations for dealing with the perception in circular reaction. (At a later stage, the child might play with the bottle and so reduce its fearsome properties of being familiar, but not further assimilable.)

In quick summary, the fourth stage might be characterized as a continuation and elaboration of the third stage; the structural changes of the third stage eventually result in a new kind of complex behavior—decomposition of old structures and reconstitution into new structures. This new process depends on two things: a sufficiently complex and interconnected data structure for chaining to occur, and a sufficiently large attention span to allow reverberations in portions of several different structures. The continued elaborations of Stage Three will finally satisfy these two prerequisites, and Stage Four is entered. The distinctions between perception, procedure, and coordination which become clear only in Stage Three are beginning to blur in Stage Four (as are the distinctions between first and second order elements in the model). These distinctions are becoming more relative and graded into one another. If the data structure could be directly examined, we might profitably grade the elements according only to the proportions of links to memory elements, of links directly from input elements, and of links directly to output elements (instead of trying to distinguish between perception, procedure, and memory). Viewed as procedure, the fourth stage data structure allows the application of familiar procedures in new situations. Viewed as perception, the fourth stage data structure allows the coordination of simpler perceptions into more complex perceptions, and the appearance of the sign; by its intercoordinations amongst its own subelements, and by its links to other structures, the fourth stage complex perception becomes greater than the sum of its parts. (Within a localized structure these fourth stage developments may occur even earlier. Within strictly visual perceptions, the whole becomes greater than the sum of its parts at about five months, as suggested by the work of Bower. At this age the child is normally thought of as being in the third stage. But this sort of confusion has been discussed before.) Finally, viewed as coordination, the fourth stage data structure allows changes that have built into them many subordinate perceptions and procedures, immediate generalizability. In short, with each change memory becomes at once more specific and more general. (Why ever would we think that specific and general were different, opposite things? The general is made up of many specifics, and the specific is included in many generalities.)

Stage V: Active Experimentation; Beginning in the Eleventh Month

The first, second, and third stages are defined by a certain level of complexity of the data structure. In the first stage, all elements are in direct contact with the environment. In the second stage, some elements are formed which have one level of elements between them and the environment, on both the input and the output side. In the third stage, elements are formed that have as many as two levels of other elements between them and the environment. Unfortunately, as this convenient distinction between levels builds up, it begins immediately to disintegrate. The same element, in different situations, may appear to be of different levels. For example, the element A in Fig. 6 is immediately linked to its own output element, one level removed from the output element of B, and two levels removed from the output element of C. Fortunately, we need only three levels of analysis anyway; input, transformation, output; perception, coordination, procedure; predecessor, occupant, successor. If, from any level of analysis, we can make contact with the next higher level and the next lower level, then from any one level we can analyze, step by step, as much of the whole as we want.

It is possible, in the first three stages of development, for the size of the attention span to limit the level of complexity of the data structure. As long as the attention span is such that only three or fewer elements may reverberate simultaneously, no new elements may be formed; the data structure stays at the lowest level of complexity. Then, when the attention span allows four elements to reverberate, the second stage is entered and first order elements are formed. At an attention span of four, the second level of elements may be inserted between the original first order elements and the input elements, but not between the original first order element and the output elements. Only with an attention span of five can new elements be formed on the output side of the original first order elements, and, thus, the third stage is entered in full generality. In the third stage, with no further increase in attention span, the level of complexity as viewed from both the input and the output side may suddenly increase indefinitely due to the phenomenon of chaining. Each new element may be added with a limited attention span, but the whole gradually builds up to a length that far exceeds the attention span. (As pointed out by Gorn (1965), this is a general phenomenon of control systems; three levels of control or analysis can be made to extend as far as desirable.) Up to the third stage, the structural complexity (measured by the greatest number of elements that can exist between any one memory element and the environment on both the input and the output sides) and the functional complexity (measured by the greatest number of different level elements that may be simultaneously reverberating) are the same. But during the third stage, the structural complexity far outstrips the functional complexity, so that, from the fourth stage on, changes in stage can be recognized only by changes in functional complexity.

The fourth stage was defined functionally as the application (reverberation or functioning) of a familiar procedure in a new situation, or as the functional decomposition of old structures (as activity flowed through their various parts) and their reconstitution by coordination and differentiation into new structures. But, in the fourth stage, decompositions are always suggested by the environment (sensory inputs bring to reverberation parts of several old structures) and reconstitutions are confirmed by the environment (the reverberating parts are successful in producing circular reaction and new sensory feedback). Now, in the fifth stage, the decompositions will come under internal control, the child will try something independently of the environment to see how it works; the child will propose or question, and the environment will confirm or answer. In the fourth stage, the child learned to remove an obstacle by striking it and only later (as opportunities from the environment presented themselves) learned to use the more suitable procedure of pushing an obstacle away. A child in the fifth stage would, upon discovering that striking had removed the obstacle, ignore the attractive goal and instead commence striking the obstacle, again observing what happened; the visual coordinations suggest various aims which the subordinate procedures of the striking procedure obediently carry out. When the results come back from the environment, they are recorded as new coordinations between the procedures just used and the perceptions just received. And, finally, the new coordinations are formed only if of interest to the visual, the striking, or the goal reaching structures, that is to say, only if novel (as yet uncoordinated) recombinations of the old structures are produced by the experiment.

The fifth stage discovery of obstacle removal by striking is not in fact reported by Piaget, 1936 (but it provides us with a convenient contrast to a similar behavior in Stage Four). The earliest example of fifth stage behavior reported by Piaget is in Observation 141. In this observation, Laurent actively explores the visual results of dropping and throwing an object; he carefully follows the trajectory of the dropped object and stares at it where it lands. He picks the object up and drops it again from a different position. If it falls near his mouth, he merely opens his mouth and tries dropping again, without sucking the object as he usually does. All this is conveniently in contrast to the dropping behavior of only a week before when his sole interest seemed to be in the sensations of letting the object slip from the hand in various ways; that was a reaction that could be carried out completely within a single complex structure—the fourth stage grasping complex with all its perceptions and subordinate procedures. The initial learning of the dropping structures is simply fourth stage differentiation. But, a week later, this structure is exercised while another structure (visual tracking procedure) is reverberating and passing these reverberations on to the dropping structure. The visual structure directs and records the results of the dropping structure. The eyes glance left, the hand follows and drops from there. The eyes follow the trajectory and coordinate the result with the still reverberating dropping structures. (Though still reverberating, the dropping structures are not producing motor outputs because activity has been lowered as a result of an orienting response to the novel experience of following the trajectory.) The eyes direct the retrieval of the object, choose a new dropping position, and watch again. The important new functional capacity in the fifth stage is this: not only are two fourth stage structures decomposed and reconstituted moment by moment as in the fourth stage, now they are decomposed: the decomposition is remembered and held in the attention span (even with no direct sensory facilitation) while one of the structures carries out its observations (that is, continues its reverberations as facilitated by the returning results from the environment), and finally when the results are in, they may be coordinated to the structure that produced them. This storage of an initial decomposition for later coordination with the result is *short term memory*. In the fourth stage, reconstitution immediately followed decomposition (as soon as the obstacle is struck, it moves; as soon as an object is dropped in a basin, the sound is heard). Now, in the fifth stage, an intervening circular reaction of some duration is carried out (the falling object is visually traced). In the fourth stage behavior, any intervening circular reaction forces the old combinations out of attention so that no new coordination is formed. As an example, only a few days before the fifth stage dropping-to-see, the child used dropping to produce a noise from a metal basin. But here the intervening retrieval of the dropped object prevents any new learning; the child merely reproduces the behavior several times allowing the basin to determine his aim, and each time starts the dropping procedure anew. The only accommodation in the dropping procedure is a functional accommodation: fitting the subordinate procedures to the location of the basin. Structural changes in the dropping structure are not made.

The basis for short term memory was laid way back in Stage Three where the second order element was reciprocally linked to the procedures it coordinated; the second order element received activity from a reverberating first order element and, if the second order element was itself reverberating, it could pass activity back to the first order element. Two reciprocally linked elements help maintain each other's reverberations. At first, this reciprocal linkage only helped; most of an element's activity still came from input elements. But, as the number of memory elements increase through Stage Four, it becomes possible for several strongly interlinked (each to every other) elements to maintain themselves in the attention span, even without sensory facilitation. Thus it becomes possible in Stage Four for the child to search for a hidden object, even after the object has been hidden and can give no sensory facilitation to an internal structure representing it (Observation 126). But even here the short term memory may have sensory facilitation (the child having seen the object hidden, need only reach in that direction); it is not until the fifth stage that short term memory is definitely independent of sensory facilitation and can even support itself in competition with an independent circular reaction. The visual tracking of a falling object cannot be said to give sensory facilitation to grasping and dropping procedures. Finally, it is very interesting that as fifth stage behavior first emerges it is accompanied by great interest in the results obtained—the child stares fascinated at the dropped object. Clearly strong orienting responses are involved, and attention span is pushed to the upper limits allowed by the present state of maturity.

An important effect of short term memory is an increase in the independence of the thought processes from sensorimotor activity. Beginning in Stage Three, sensory inputs must pass reverberations through a level of perceptual elements before reaching the central coordinations (See Fig. 5). Thus, while the orienting response places an emphasis on the novel experience, the complexity of the data structure begins to demand a certain familiarity for circular reaction (from input through output) to proceed. Now, in Stage Five, the sensory inputs must not only pass through a level of perception, they must either be strong enough to compete with self-supporting short term memory (by raising the activity in some nonreverberating element as high as the activities in the reverberating short term memory) or they might simply give additional activity to one or another element involved in short term memory and so influence the central processes. Otherwise, sensory inputs are filtered out. They must now be both structurally familiar and functionally relevant (or they must be of unusual intensity). Not only must they pass activity to perceptual elements, but those perceptual elements must be already on attention.

It should be possible to construct a diagram of the structures involved in fifth stage behavior. Such an attempt is made in Fig. 7. Here each element is rather complex and actually represents a number of roughly parallel and interconnected perceptions, subordinated procedures, and coordinations. Also, each link between these complex elements represents a number of links between different subelements. As an example, the reaching procedures have been amplified somewhat. Finally, each of the complex elements is facilitated by a number of input elements and facilitates a number of output elements, but none of this is shown. The throwing, or dropping-to-see-fall reaction will again be analyzed because it is in this reaction that the role of short term memory is clearest. (Piaget, 1936, gives many other examples, but in most of them the feedback from the environment is immediate, as when the end of a stick moves at the same time the hand grasping it moves. In these cases, it is a goal, a perception of a desirable object, that takes up extra room on the attention span and directs the persistent attempts to use the stick.)

We should begin with an analysis of the fourth stage behavior of dropping-to-feel-drop. Here we find the child exercising the coordination between arm positioning procedures and the grasping and ungrasping procedures. These coordinations were formed when the child was fumbling around trying to grasp an object and it slipped from his hand. The new sensation of the object slipping, rolling, falling from his hand causes an orienting response; attention span is increased, new elements are brought to reverberation and coordinated to the elements that were already reverberating. When an object is dropped from the hand, the sensory facilitation that the object provided to the grasping procedures comes to an end and reverberation in the grasping procedures fails. This results in a new element coming to reverberation, and a likely candidate is a visual element; the visual system locks onto the dropped object and, through the hand-eye coordination, directs its retrieval. But this retrieval is carried out only because of the failure of the old structures which have ceased reverberations; therefore, there can be no coordination formed between the visual system's record of the place where the dropped object lands and the dropping system's record of the movement that made the object land where it did. The child cannot improve his aim. (In fact, the child can position his hand in visual contact with a target and then drop, but he cannot look at the target and thereby know how to position his hand or aim a throw.) Only after retrieval can the dropping be resumed, and, when it is, the position of the hand and arms at the end of the retrieval determines, in part, the new drop. Also, the same small attention span that prevented visual tracking until failure of the grasping and dropping, may now prevent dropping until the visual tracking ceases. In any event, the hand-eye coordination for reaching for an object, and the dropping coordination for releasing the object interact only in alternation and not in coordination.

In the fifth stage, the child is not so interested in the sensations of dropping; the already established dropping coordination of the fourth stage assimilates these. The sensation feeds some of its activity into the already reverberating elements and is partly expected—no orienting response occurs. If, however, the falling object is seen, this is a new and unexpected sensation. An orienting response is made and visual coordinations begin reverberating. Now, if the attention span is large enough, the visual tracking may proceed while interlinked elements of the dropping coordination maintain one another's reverberations. In such a case, the visual results of the drop may be coordinated to the still reverberating structures that caused the drop and the broken line structure of Fig. 7 would be formed. In a subsequent attempt, the child might inspect his environment visually, locate the place where his last drop ended, and, without looking at his hand, direct a new drop in that direction. Not only is a new kind of coordination now possible between action and deferred result, but there is also a new kind of directed functioning. With increased attention span, the visual tracking procedures fixed on a target may arouse various movements of the out of sight arm by passing activity through the hand-eye coordinations, and if the dropping coordinations are still reverberating, a new drop may result. Thus, the activity of the visual system introduces variations in the dropping

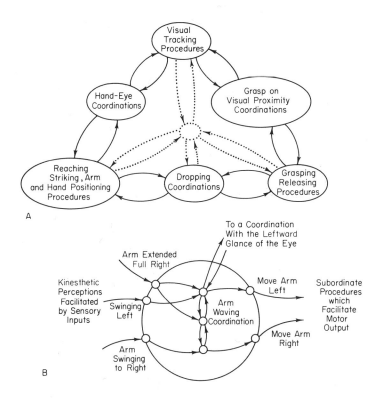

Fig. 7. Active experimentation. A. Overall structure. B. Some details of the complex procedures of the hand and arm.

system and the result is active, internally directed experimentation. Visual stimuli become signs that alter the functioning of another system. The dropping coordination is differentiated by its interaction with, and effect on the visual system; throwing is discovered. Each variation introduced by the activity from the visual system results in an experiment, and each experiment that gives interesting visual effects (that is, unexpected visual effects) produces a new, slightly differentiated dropping coordination or procedure.

Without detailed analysis, a few more of Piaget's observations can be cited which give some evidence of short term memory. In Observation 146, Jacqueline presses on the edge of a box which tilts up and falls down. In an attempt to reproduce the result, she restores the box to its original distance from herself and presses it again. It would seem possible for the original location of the box to have been a short term memory of the fact that the arm was extended some distance when the first press on the box was made. Then, even though the arm has been flexed in the meantime, in reproducing the result the child pushes the box as far as possible and then presses on it again. There is nothing left in the environment to suggest the original location of the box and we must assume some form of memory has directed the reconstruction of the original conditions (or we can throw the Observation out as experimental accident). Whether this memory is a permanent change in the data structure, or a residual reverberation in the old, is very difficult to tell. No doubt there is something of both. Several minutes later, with a new object, the child throws it as far as possible before pressing on it to make it tilt up; distance is definitely part of the new coordination. In Observation 158, Lucienne uses a stick to bring an object within reaching distance. Here the visual tracking procedures and a striking procedure have already been coordinated and differentiated by the past use of the stick for striking objects. Now these procedures are exercised, but with some goal in mind: that of bringing the object nearer to a point in the visual field that can be reached. Some short term memory of an earlier attempt to reach for the object could be actively influencing the striking movements of the arm to bring the object in reach. Something other than external stimuli is directing the movements and rather than label this something as intention, motive, goal, or will, it seems least mysterious to call it short term memory.

The difficulty in distinguishing between short term memory and long term memory is partly because the interpretation in the formal model views short term memory as merely a functional aspect of long term (or structural) memory. There is no short term functional memory without (perhaps previously established) long term structural memory. Where Hebb showed that structures of interconnected neurons could reverberate for short periods of time even after the initial stimulations had died away (OS3), in Stage Five we are only discovering that reverberations of reverberations can also last beyond the stimulations that began them. Hebb described this as a phase cycle; reverberations drifting back and forth in a set of interconnected assemblies. A group of interconnected assemblies behave in much the same manner as a single assembly, but, now, with a longer time scale and a greater total activity. A group of assemblies can be differentiated when one of the member assemblies becomes coordinated to another structure outside of the group. Everything that can happen to an assembly has an analogue that happens to a group of assemblies. Perhaps herein lie the clues as to the nature of the cell assembly whose inner workings are like the inner workings of a group of assemblies. And, perhaps, herein lie the clues as to the course of development of short term memory which behaves like an individual assembly, only, now, with some internal variations we cannot ignore, a single activity is not enough.

To quickly summarize the developments of the fifth stage: there are two of them. First is the appearance of short term memory and the capacity for coordinating actions with deferred results. For the first time, a real independence from the environment seems possible in the function of a self-supporting group of assemblies. But only one group of assemblies can function at a time; attention span is not large enough to accommodate two. The other important development of this stage is the appearance of active experimentation; no longer content to explore an object and apply what procedures are available, the child is now interested in exploring a procedure by applying another procedure to it. The external object is replaced by an internal short term memory as director of experimental activity. The implications of one procedure for another are systematically worked out as each subordinate procedure is applied and the results, if interesting, are recorded as a new coordination to the other procedure. Both developments of the fifth stage seem to depend on an increase in the attention span so that one fully functioning system can interact with parts of another (rather than one after the other, and rather than two undifferentiated procedures functioning together). Also, the increase in memory to memory links allows one system to wrest control of the other from the environment.

Stage VI: Mental Recombinations; Beginning in the Second Year

With the continued formation of memory elements, the consequent increase in the proportion of memory-to-memory links, and the maturation of the attention span, the child finally is able to maintain two different short term memory structures in the attention span without direct sensory facilitation. In the fifth stage, the child could think of something to try (that is, reverberations in one structure could pass on to another structure thereby suggesting an experiment, a proposed change in the second structure), but he could only discover the results by actively carrying out the experiment on the environment. In the sixth stage, the child can both think of an experiment and foresee its results without recourse to the environment. This is made possible because of the elaborations that were perhaps actively discovered in the fifth stage; both structures have already been differentiated according to the interesting results they produce in each other. An experiment is proposed by one structure, and the result is already given by the coordinations to the other structure. If the result is of no interest to the first structure (if the internal feedback from the second structure does not support the reverberations that made the proposal), then the activities in the first structure may be changed slightly by the feedback and a new pattern of reverberation is passed back to the second structure for evaluation. Such an interaction may continue without observable motor activity until the two structures have, between them, proposed and confirmed an experiment or solution. Then the mutual facilitations between the two may build up the activities of the reverberating elements to the point where motor action commences. For the first time, behavior is observed, and the structure which has been observed to be functioning longest appears to have used the second structure with foresight, intention, and invention.

Not only must the two structures be sufficiently complex and differentiated, they must also be capable of a certain degree of independence from each other. Thus, the first structure which passes reverberations on to the second, does not immediately compromise with the second and base its own reverberations on those of the second. The first structure is receiving facilitations from someplace else and it is this additional source of reverberations which allows the first structure its relative independence from the second. Or, alternatively, the first structure may be much better intercoordinated and able to maintain its own reverberations. In addition, the second structure is not passively receiving activity from the first, it is actively evaluating the activity from the first element in the context of its own reverberations which may in turn be supported by other structures. It is this relative independence of the first and second structures which strongly suggests a central core of mutually facilitating elements in each structure. There are two short term memory structures, although in the early parts of Stage Six they are still partly dependent on sensory input and a mutual interaction. (On finer analysis, the stages of Piaget are much more continuous than the prototypes used to distinguish them.)

An example of Stage Six invention is the use of a stick to bring a desirable object within grasping distance. In Stage Five, this was done by experimental interaction with the environment; the child moved the stick one way, observed the results, and if the results were of interest and of value (if they made reaching easier by giving further facilitation to the visual component of reaching), they were repeated. In Observation 177, Laurent who has already observed the effects of the stick in moving distant objects, but who has never used the stick to retrieve an object, invents the use of the stick as a reaching aid. A crust of bread is placed before Laurent who reaches for it but fails. A stick is also presented to Laurent who now grasps it and reaches for the bread with it. Being held in the middle, it doesn't reach. Laurent puts it down and reaches directly for the bread again, and fails again. Now Laurent picks up the stick again, but at one of its ends. He succeeds in touching it to the bread, and after a few seconds delay moves it to the side gently and finally directly to him. Subsequently, Laurent is able to immediately grasp a convenient stick and use it to draw toys to himself.

A child in the fifth stage would perhaps grasp the stick and strike the bread crust with it, thus only applying an undifferentiated structure to the object out of reach. Only then, after seeing the object move closer, would the child begin to actively experiment to find the movements that would bring it within reach. In contrast, Laurent has grasped the stick and immediately tried to put it in contact with the bread. Succeeding in this, with only one initial mistake, he draws it directly to himself. Laurent has the prevision necessary to select the proper procedure and apply it. The attempt to reach the bread with the unaided hand has perhaps conditioned the visual system to fix on a reachable point in the visual field. Then, the visual system might pull away from this goal structure embedded in it, fix on the stick, and the mental recombination described above would take place. The goal of moving the bread closer to the point where the hand was seen to reach is the independent source of reverberations that allows the visual system to judge which of the movements of the stick will be most useful. Laurent has definitely maintained his interest in the bread and his knowledge of where it must be moved while he is busy looking at the stick and retrieving it. The short term memory of the goal to be achieved interacts with the coordinations of the stick (which were learned earlier) to select the appropriate movement. (Even though wrong, moving gently to the side is certainly more appropriate than striking.) Not only is a short term memory maintained on attention, but, also, a rather complex interaction between it and a structure that is receiving sensory facilitation is carried out. (The presence of the stick in the hand may help to maintain the coordinations formed by past experience with the stick.) While we cannot say for certain that two independent short term memories are held in attention, there is certainly a greater number of elements reverberating than was the case in Stage Five. In the simplified diagram of Fig. 8, the short term memory is represented as a group of mutually facilitating elements from various other structures in the diagram. While these elements support each other in attention, the hand-eye coordinations and the reaching-grasping coordinations are exercised. The stick is retrieved because it facilitates old coordinations that once produced changes in the visual field, changes which are now recognized as useful because of the discrepancy between the location of the bread and the farthest reach of the hand. Perhaps the variations in glance from bread to outstretched hand is the same as the variations in glance produced by past swinging of the stick. Once the stick is in the hand, but before motor output is produced, the residual reverberations in the short term memory produce higher activities in some visual and manual procedures than others. It is this variation in activity that influences the selection of movements to be made with the stick. At this stage there is a definite separation of goal (bring the bread in reach) and means of reaching that goal (use the stick). (Alas, my ignorance prevents me from putting more detail into Fig. 8. The inner workings of the complex elements shown are certainly not evident from Piaget's (1936) observations and the great number of individual motor movements precludes an analysis here. I am only taking aim and suggesting that it could be done within the framework of the model. Again, a more complete knowledge of the actual procedures and coordinations possessed by Laurent is necessary.)

In Observation 180 another example of invention is given. Lucienne is trying to remove a watch chain from a matchbox. The matchbox is slightly open so the chain inside is visible but cannot come out. Lucienne tries to grasp the chain to pull it out; she puts her finger in the slit and succeeds in getting to the rest of the chain. Then her father replaces the chain without her seeing, but this time reduces the slit even more. Lucienne puts her finger into the slit, but fails

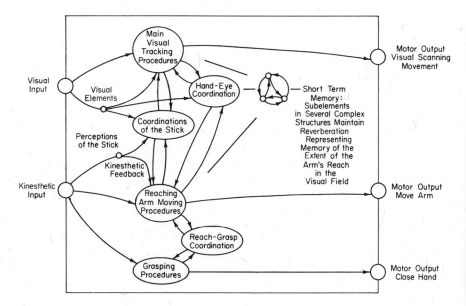

Fig. 8. The development of short term memory in an interconnected group of elements.

to retrieve the chain. She pauses, looks at the slit attentively, opens and closes her mouth slightly, and then wider and wider. She then puts her finger into the slit in the matchbox, pulls it open, and finally takes the chain. Here we can see the mental working out of a solution (with a bit of motor action accompanying it). Perhaps the feel of the slit in the matchbox reminded Lucienne of her own mouth and previous exercise of the grasping and sucking coordination. Opening her mouth wider, she could reach her teeth with her finger. (Or, as Piaget suggests, in playing with her father, Lucienne learned to imitate him when he opened his mouth.) Lucienne almost makes this rediscovery without external aid and promptly uses it to make the slit wider. Here again there seems to be a short term memory of the chain in the box interacting with another short term memory of the hand at the mouth. Again, an earlier discovery is recalled and immediately applied without external experimentation or hesitation (unless we are to consider Lucienne's mouth opening as something more than a motor overflow of the mental processes).

In Observation 181 Lucienne tries to kneel before a stool, but finds that it slides away from her. She gets up and puts the stool against a sofa so she can finally kneel. Not only is there a persistent intention to use the stool to kneel, but when it slides away there is a failure of circular reaction. Perhaps the resulting orienting response could bring to reverberation elements that were associated with the kneeling procedure and which represented a sensorimotor image of the steady stool. Lucienne could then set about recreating this steadiness with whatever her experiences have taught her. Here is the second relatively stable short term memory representing the procedures for steadying the stool. Without disrupting the first short term memory of kneeling, this second memory is strong enough to impose itself on the environment and rearrange the situation—Lucienne moves the stool to a place where she perhaps knows she has used it before. Then, only after this interaction with the environment is completed does the old intention of kneeling by the stool finally express itself.

Because the entire process of experimentation can now be internalized, analysis of any depth becomes impossible. Without a complete history of all a child's experiences, it is impossible to know what is going on. We are reduced to making hypotheses. However, the formal model we have been using accounts for this internalization of the thought processes. Another difficulty at this point is the rapidly increasing complexity of the procedures with all their subordinate procedures, perceptions, and coordinations. Fortunately, it seems that the basic unit of internalized thought is the short term memory which consists of a group of mutually facilitating elements. If we can shift gears to this higher level of organization, there will be fewer individual units to worry about. And all our accumulated understanding of the functioning of the individual assembly in relation to others gives us an immediate understanding of how the group of elements will function as a short term memory, even though we are unable to obtain direct behavioral evidence of the details of this internalized process. Let us therefore review the course of development before it finally disappears entirely from our sight.

Summary of the Sensorimotor Period

The central characteristic of development is the progressive independence of the child's thought processes from direct sensory and motor influence. Beginning at Stage One, there is obligatory obedience to the "wired-in" reflexes, such as there are. Amongst the earliest maturing reflexes are the sucking and grasping reflexes. These have a fairly specific motor output for a fairly specific sensory input. Other specific reflexes include the sneeze, the cough, and the swallow, all of which tend not to reinforce themselves through circular reaction with the environment and tend to remain undeveloped. There are also many localized orienting reflexes (not to be confused with the generalized central orienting response) which direct the sensory receptors towards any low to moderate stimulation, and there are many localized defense reflexes which withdraw sensory receptors from very strong stimulation. Finally, through the central orienting response, almost any input is linked to certain autonomic reflexes regulating heart rate, respiration, and many other somatic functions. Through all these reflexes, just about any sensory input results in some arousal and subsequent motor response unless prevented by the functioning of another system of circular reactions. With reflexes, a given stimulation always produces, with little variation, a rather precise response or a very general and undifferentiated orienting response. There is no internal function beyond a coarse regulation of the transmission of activity from input through reflex links to output. The structure of the model at this stage is shown in Fig. 9A where the topology of the input and output elements has been rearranged from the earlier diagrams to match more closely the paired arrangement found in the human body. Given a spatial pattern of sensory stimulation, there is some specific or else general and undifferentiated output, and little more until the input pattern is changed (as might be done by the motor response itself). The only way to change from one reflexive circular reaction on a certain set of input and output elements to a reaction on another set of elements is through kinesthetic feedback or other sensory stimulations from objects in the environment.

Beginning with Stage Two, the first level of elements is formed; certain input patterns come to give fairly well defined output responses, depending on the past use of the reflexes in the first stage. Successful reflexive circular reactions increase the responsiveness of the reflexes to the input patterns produced by the circular reaction. At the same time, the patterns of motor output that produce good circular reaction are strengthened and more easily reproduced. This is the first form of recognition and memory because the new patterns of reaction are dependent on the past experience of the child—they are not automatically produced by maturation. Hebb's (1949) model hypothesized an assembly of neurons differentiated out of the old reflexive systems and formed into a separate unit that would respond to the learned input pattern by passing activity on to the associated output pattern. Now, given a familiar input pattern, a learned output pattern results. Further, the child can, to some degree, be trained to associate or coordinate input-output patterns that cross the boundaries of the individual reflex systems. Still, the behavior of the child is entirely dependent on its input stimulation (including much kinesthetic feedback from the body which is not observable as external stimulation from the environment); a specific input elicits a specific output, and the nervous system in yoke with the rest of the body produces spontaneous circular reaction. The only advance over the first stage is that the input and output patterns of the circular reactions are better defined and differentiated: more reliably and predictably aroused sometimes, more variable and internally conditioned at other times, and dependent on past experience and learning. But, the child cannot yet, of its own accord, activate just any output patterns beyond those defined by reflex link or memory element, and aroused by current sensory inputs. At best, the child can only choose from amongst the alternatives presented by the environment, the ones best suited to his particular structures; volition is limited to judging which structure is most relevant, most active. As shown in Fig. 9B, there are still no paths for the flow of activity except those beginning at input and eventually ending at output. Input activity quickly ends as output activity and can only reenter the system through external mediaries.

In Stage Three, with the next level of assemblies, we find that the learned input-output associations of the second stage are themselves coordinated, so that the input of one association may produce the output of a second association, even without the input normally required for the second. The same process which appears as the coordination of separate structures also appears as the differentiation into parts of each individual structure. For the first time, some memory elements may be better linked to input elements and appear as perceptions while other memory elements may be better linked to output elements and appear as procedures. The appearance of reciprocal links between memory elements produces more sustained functioning of any one structure, and the additional elements producing differentiation and coordination allow greater choice and variation to the internal processes. What happened to the reflexes of the first stage now happens to the coordinations of the second stage. An increased attention span and additional internal facilitation provided by the second order assemblies allows, finally, two different reflex systems to function simultaneously. And, it should be noted, the new second order elements are completely general just as the original first order elements were; in different contexts or from different points of view, the same assembly may appear to function like a perception in recognizing the familiar, like a coordination in having connections to several other different structures, and like a procedure in having an effect on the exact pattern of motor response. In Fig. 9C, the coordinated structure on the left could with very little change be part of the larger structure on the right (the central element stays the same, and the coordinated elements become the subordinate perceptions of the larger structure).

In Stage Four, the second level, or derived, assemblies become more numerous. They allow a short circuiting between two remote structures which are only indirectly connected through a third structure. In Fig. 9D, starting at the center procedure, activity may pass as usual to the procedure on the left which functions but fails to achieve circular reaction. This is unexpected and more elements are brought to reverberation. The procedure on the right, already receiving some sensory facilitation perhaps, begins functioning and produces a change in the environment which even more strongly facilitates the original procedure on the left. Thus, reverberations pass from one procedure indirectly to another with the aid of an internal mediary and an external support. The formation of a new direct coordination between the left and right procedures is mediated by the procedure in the middle. But the limited attention span allows only a small amount of reverberation at a time, and to have simultaneous reverberations in the right and left procedures required sensory facilitation from the environment both in selecting a new procedure after failure of the one on the left, and in giving sensory feedback from the functioning of the rightmost procedure to the leftmost procedure. And, of course, both the left and right procedures are coordinated with all their other connections (not shown in Fig. 9D) to subordinate and coordinate structures now implicitly available to each other.

In Stage Five, short term memory becomes an important factor and allows new functional capacities for the child. Even in the first stage there were two forms of memory, a permanent structural memory of elements and links, and a transitory functional memory of reverberations and activities in the elements. With increasing complexity of the structural memory and increasing size of the attention span, functional memory is able to maintain itself for longer and longer periods of time, and with greater and greater independence from direct sensory influence. Finally, in the fifth stage, a small group of mutually facilitating elements is able to maintain its own reverberations independently of, and even in competition with, reverberations in other structures. The short term memory may be held to the side while other structures continue functioning in direct circular reaction with the environment. Then, at appropriate moments (when the patterns of activity and reverberation allow), the short term memory may influence the functioning of the circular reaction (as when an internally determined goal influences the course of action), or the functioning of the circular reaction may influence the short term memory functionally (as when the short term memory reestablishes contact with the environment and begins its own circular reaction with variations induced by the other structure), or, even structurally (as when new coordinations are formed with elements of the short term memory although the short term memory does not actually begin circular reaction with the environment). Behavior is the same as in Stage Four, but, now, with a new persistence and recurrence of a particular procedure which appears as deliberate experimentation and interest in the procedure itself. In Fig. 9E, the structure is identical to that of Fig. 9D except for the additional internal facilitations provided by the group of elements attached to one of the procedures. In contrast to Stage Four, the procedure on the right keeps recurring, with variations induced by the middle structure, and in competition with the environmentally facilitated structure on the left.

At last, in Stage Six, the simultaneous functioning of two different short term memory structures terminates the child's dependence on environmental support for his thought processes. At first this is but a tenuous independence; environmental influence is not far away and those memory structures which take activity from input elements will still be the strongest. Also, two "different"

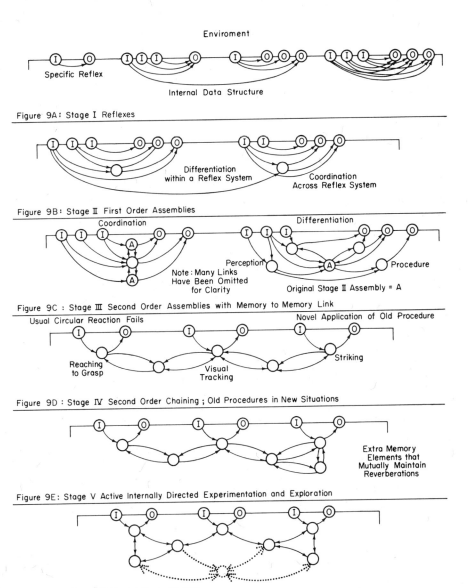

Figure 9A: Stage I Reflexes

Figure 9B: Stage II First Order Assemblies

Figure 9C : Stage III Second Order Assemblies with Memory to Memory Link

Figure 9D : Stage IV Second Order Chaining ; Old Procedures in New Situations

Figure 9E: Stage V Active Internally Directed Experimentation and Exploration

Figure 9F : Stage VI Mental Recombination

Fig. 9. A. Stage I, reflexes. B. Stage II, first order assemblies. C. Stage III, second order assemblies with memory to memory links. D. Stage IV, second order chaining: old procedures in new situations. E. Stage V, active, internally directed experimentation and exploration. F. Stage VI, mental recombination.

short term memories that in fact have a few elements in common will more easily function together. But, even in its earliest forms, Stage Six behavior is a clear advance over any of the previous stages: the child can now select a goal, persist in pursuing that goal even without sensory contact with the goal, and, besides, select a means for reaching the goal and apply the means preadjusted to the situation. In full blown Stage Six behavior, the child may select both goal and means without direct sensory support (for example the child who is after a toy that is hidden under a sofa and who goes looking for a stick that cannot yet be seen), but for a long while some environmental support of the two structures is necessary. As diagrammed in Fig. 9F, a goal structure on the left arouses a means structure on the right (perhaps through common elements) and the resulting interaction between them (an interaction, in part, depending on and adjusted to the sensory inputs) initiates a coordinated circular reaction with the structure in the middle. If the child guessed right, the circular reaction of the goal structure on the left will then be successful. Finally, in Stage Six, the possibility of a purely memory linked element arises. At all earlier stages, sensory and motor elements were required to maintain reverberations, and any elements formed would most likely include at least some links from input elements and to output elements. With the reverberations of two different short term memories, a coordination might be formed between them that has no connections to input or output elements, the short term memories having taken up the whole of the attention span. Reverberations may pass from one short term memory to another until two short term memories (from two different but already coordinated predecessors) are reverberating that have never reverberated together before. A purely imaginative coordination, a new *third order element* is formed (making four levels in all; zeroth order input and output, first order memory with input and output links only, second order memory with some memory to memory links, and third order with only memory to memory links). The structural effect of these third order elements may be a pronounced short circuiting between remote elements, as suggested in Fig. 9F.

The child at age two still has a good ten years of development before reaching the capacity for purely formal thought which we value so highly. I will hazard a guess that none of the developments of these next ten years will be as surprising as, or much different from the developments of the first two we have just reviewed. Shifting gears slightly, we might expect a gradual increase in the number of short term memory units; otherwise, the function, structure, and development of short term memory is implicit in our understanding of the assemblies that make up the short term memory. With two units of short term memory there is a ready analogy with the first stage of sensorimotor development; again, only two units may function at a time, still regulated by the central processes, but now with the entire circular reaction internalized. With three units there is a clear separation of the levels of analysis; input, learned transformation, and output in the sensorimotor Stage Two; by analogy, the child of three and older is able to separate and independently vary the three levels of starting stage, transformation, and goal state. This might correspond to Piaget's period of concrete operations. At this level of development, the child's thought processes and representations of the external world are identical and hence confused. Finally, with six units of short term memory, the adolescent can hold in functional memory a three level representation of the external world and also a three level abstract representation to guide his thought processes. Analogies can be abstracted and analyzed without changing the concrete representation in which they occur. Changes can be made in the representation without automatic extension to the abstraction. New concrete representations can be quickly built up by using formal structures as models. In short, the end of the process is analogous to Stage Six of the sensorimotor period where two structures could be maintained, and independently of one another. At the highest level of intelligence, a situation is taken from the environment and internalized as concrete short term memories. These are coordinated to abstractions of other concrete images, and those abstractions are then used to select some abstract transformation which is immediately interpreted as a coordinated concrete transformation (procedure) and applied.

All of which suggests a great deal more than will be done in the rest of this book. Instead, in the remaining chapters, a few important sensorimotor systems will be traced in greater detail through the six stages of early development. Then evidence from other areas of psychological research will be loosely coordinated with the model developed here. After that, the model will be used to give interpretations of language and conceptualization. And, finally, a method of computer simulation will be outlined. Instead of continuing with a step by step deductive analysis of Piaget's observations, the rest of this book will be devoted to making some contact with a variety of different viewpoints in an attempt to provide some inductive support for the hypothesis so far developed. (In fact it has taken me four years of puzzling and wondering to convince myself that I might some day begin to understand the first year of the development of intelligence, let alone the rest in 44 years, I doubt that I will be sufficiently temerarious to write this much next year.)

CHAPTER 3
MAJOR SENSORMOTOR SYSTEMS

The Visual System

The reflexive functioning of the visual system in human infants a few days after birth has been studied by Salapatek (1966). The very simplified diagram in Fig. 10 will help to interpret his findings in terms of the model developed here. Behaviorally, a very important part of this system is the musculature which moves the eye back and forth in a scanning motion. This is the only function of the visual system that we can observe externally and it is the first function which allows the infant to incorporate visual stimulations into a circular reaction.

Even in the absence of visual stimulation, the scanning system may function through kinesthetic feedback. When the eye is turned to the left, the muscles on the right are stretched and begin giving sensory facilitation to an automatic reflex which will pull the eye back to the right. Symmetrically, the muscles on the left will then pull the eye back to the left and the result will be a constant reflexive scanning motion of the eye back and forth in the horizontal plane. There is also a pair of muscles that pull the eye up and down in a vertical scan, but this is omitted in Fig. 10 for simplicity.

The amplitude of the scanning motions will depend on the current status of the attention span. If there are a number of elements on the attention span with high activity, then it will take larger displacements for sensory feedback from the stretching of the muscles to reach a high enough activity to break into reverberations and activate the reflexive motor response. If the child is sleeping, with a very small attention span and high activities in those elements that are reverberating, then the stretch may never become strong enough to produce a response. On the other hand, if the attention span is large and the activity of the elements on it are small, then the activity of the kinesthetic feedback may quickly reach a level sufficient to reverberate and produce a response. When the response is produced it will be of a smaller amplitude because of the lower activity passed by links at a high attention span. Thus, when the child is alert or has produced an orienting response, the scans will be much more localized.

In all his experiments, Salapatek (1968) found that the presence of a figure in the visual field significantly reduced the dispersion of the scan and localized it in the vicinity of the figure. This could be interpreted as follows: as the visual image of the figure moves toward the fovea at the center of the eye, the total activity in the visual input elements rises because of the increasing density of receptors towards the fovea. If the visual input elements were not already reverberating, the stimulus provokes an orienting response and reduces the scanning motions. In addition, activity from the left or right side of the retina facilitates, respectively, the right or left components of the scanning reflexes. Thus, the scan will tend to drift onto the visual image and localize in its vicinity. But the infant with an immature attention span and accompanying high activities in reverberating elements will constantly overshoot the visual image; he cannot yet make small enough scanning motions to fix on the visual image. Still, each time the visual image sweeps nearer the fovea, an increase in the activity of the nonreverberating visual input elements will result, and the orienting response will be maintained; scanning will remain localized.

According to the model developed in the previous chapter, the orienting response should end (or be countered by a rebound defense response) when a stimulus succeeds in bringing an element to reverberation. For many of Salapatek's (1968) subjects this seemed never to occur. For more than a minute, these infants would continue to localize their scanning in the vicinity of the figure. It is as if the visual image never brought any elements to reverberation; perhaps these infants had a more immature attention span which required higher activities to allow reverberation than could be attained by the visual stimuli Salapatek used. These infants sensed something was there and oriented toward it, but they could never recognize it (or find it). Some of the infants did in fact localize their scan on one portion of a large figure and then move away from this portion and localize on another. These infants perhaps brought input elements to reverberation, stopped orienting, and drifted off to another portion of the figure.

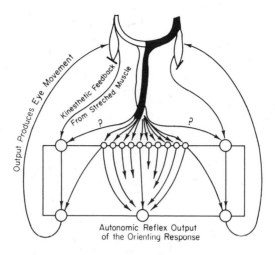

Fig. 10. The visual system at the reflex level.

Finally, Salapatek's findings suggest that the infant's gaze is more attracted to black areas of the visual field than to white areas, and is generally attracted to lines and edges. This would seem to be consistent with the following hypothesis: the primitive input elements of the visual system consist of brightness detectors, darkness detectors, and line or edge detectors. Any visual image that activates one or more of these detectors may result in an orienting response and localization of the scan near the detected stimulus. However, if the brightness detectors are the earliest maturing (if their maximal activities are rather high at birth), they may be brought to reverberation most easily; when the fovea enters a bright area of the figure, a defense response may result and the scanning movements increase in size. Thus, while attracted to a white figure, once there, the scan is larger than for a black figure. (In addition, evidence from physiology suggests the existence of line detectors, for example, Hubel and Wiesel's work with kittens and the existence of darkness detectors; the optic nerve is quite active even in the dark.) Also, Salapatek found the horizontal scan to be more dispersed than the vertical—its muscles are larger and, perhaps, its activities are higher and can reach reverberation more easily.

The retina has a great many rods and cones in it; we might well expect a similar number of primitive input elements. However, any individual cell in the retina, and, probably, any individual detector of which it is a part, has a rather small activity—it could never bring to reverberation a very large pattern of neural activity by itself. Only by combining a large number of these tiny elements could enough activity be put together to break into reverberation on the infant's immature attention span. In the limit, it might take the combined activity of all the primitive inputs to produce a response. Only as attention span matures and experience differentiates the single complex element into subsets of its component parts will the system eventually reach the capacity to detect, recognize, and respond to visual stimuli in their finest detail. Maybe an innate form of perceptual constancy lies in the undifferentiated nature of the many parallel input-output reflexes of the visual system. A visual image of a moving object is only a slight variation of the total activity of the one complex input element. Even though input element activities are changing, the summed activities and their output effect may remain fairly stable.

The formation of the first level cell assemblies will differentiate the complex visual element. For example, in Fig. 11, a line in the visual field may sweep back and forth across the retina activating all those line detectors that respond to a line of that particular orientation. In this case, the activity of the complex visual element is exactly the same as the activity of all its component parts; if the activities are high enough to admit some parts of the complex visual element to attention, then the formation of memory elements begins. Any element formed will have links, not from every element of the complex visual element, but only from those line detectors which reached reverberation. Thus, the line detectors of a particular orientation may be differentiated out of the complex by virtue of their links to the new element. From now on, a line of that orientation may have a perceptual constancy dependent on continuing reverberations in the element. Of course the element may have connections with the scanning reflexes (whose functioning may have caused the line to sweep the retina). In the future, a glance to the left will not cause surprise at the sudden movement of a line in the visual field to the right because the memory element whose activity comes from that line will merely continue to receive activity from the line, but now through a different set of detectors. The balance of activity between reverberating elements and nonreverberating elements will not change. Similarly, if the line begins to move independently of the scanning motions, it will still be assimilated by the same element and recognized (or ignored) as the same line. Perceptual constance is innate in the complex visual element and develops by differentiation.

While the visual field is being differentiated by the first order elements, it is recombined by coordinations between these elements. Thus, a Stage Three coordination between the element that differentiates the vertical line detectors and the element that differentiates the horizontal line detectors might represent a primitive recognition of a cross. This new element displays perceptual constance just as the earlier ones did, and it also displays perceptual unity— crossed horizontal and vertical lines represent a new entity different from either component. Finally, it must be remembered that this new element does not only receive links from the earlier cell assemblies but, also, directly from the primitive input detectors (see Fig. 3); it also represents further differentiation, and in the presence of a cross will have a higher activity than either of the vertical or

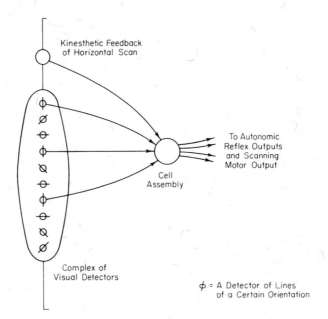

Fig. 11. Differentiation of the Complex of Usual Elements.

horizontal line assemblies. Where the perceptual constance of a moving cross is innate, this model suggests that the perceptual unity of the cross is learned. This latter suggestion is in agreement with Bower's study of perceptual unity in infancy.

A certain error appears. Since the coordination representing the cross receives facilitation from the detectors which also give facilitation to the vertical line assembly, the visual image of a vertical line may equally well arouse both the cross assembly and the vertical line assembly! This is the Gestalt concept of completion. The child who has learned to recognize a cross, may, on seeing a vertical line, look for an expected horizontal line. In any case, the conditions under which the cross assembly was constructed would not be the same as those under which the vertical line assembly was constructed. Only some of the detectors would be in common.

Only after the third stage does the whole become different from the sum of its parts. Once formed, the cross coordination will receive greater activity from a visual image of a cross than either of its components. The cross assembly is more likely to reach reverberation and even crowd out the simpler line assemblies. Now, any coordinations formed while a visual image of a cross is on the retina, may have links to the cross assembly, but not to either of the line assemblies. Learning to respond in some way to a cross will not generalize too well to either of the cross's components. And, conversely, coordinations formed with the line assemblies will not generalize too well to the cross since reverberations in the cross assembly tend to suppress the line assemblies by competition. The line assemblies fail to reverberate, and no activity is passed on to responses that have been coordinated to them. Furthermore, if some response is coordinated to each of the lines, it will not generalize too well to even another figure which is not a cross but composed of the two lines, for example, a right angle. Since the two line assemblies pass activity on to the coordination representing the cross, the presentation of the right angle will bring to reverberation the two line assemblies (assuming the right angle has not yet been learned), and their old coordination of the cross results in an increase in activity passed to nonreverberation elements—the nearly recognized cross produces an orienting response which halts or confuses the learned response that was to be generalized to the right angle. This is in agreement with Bower's study of heterogeneous summation where infants only began to respond differently to the part and to the whole between the third and fifth month. At the same time, it must be emphasized that generalization does not become impossible, only less likely.

In Stage Four, the child may be able to use chaining or signals to direct his activity. Here we found the earliest searching behavior when an object disappeared. The direct sensory inputs from the visual field after the object's disappearance may be used as signals that the object is still there. In terms of the model, the activity from the detectors is passed through the perceptual elements that recognize the images in the field and through coordinations to some of the elements that had been receiving activity from the vanished image. Still, some form of sensory support is necessary. In Stage Five, with the capacity for short term memory, the persistence of the "perception" becomes at last independent of sensory support. The age given by Piaget (1936) for Stage Five and, hence, our schedule for the development of object-permanence matches the experimentally determined figure given by Bower in his study of existence constancy—roughly the end of the first year.

Finally, to carry a thing to its end (and new beginning), it is only well into the sixth stage that Piaget reports children's dreams for the first time. Of course the observational difficulties make any accurate date for the commencement of dreams impossible. But is does seem the capacity for two independent but interacting short term memories is a prerequisite for the ability to conjure up visual images without sensory support and recombine them into completely invented fantasies.

The Auditory and Vocal Systems

The exact nature of the sensory analyzers (detectors, input elements) of the auditory system is perhaps less clear than the nature of the visual analyzers. However, the auditory system is sensitive to frequency and intensity, and we know that any brief sample of noise may be characterized on these two dimensions. By analogy to the development of the visual system, we might hypothesize that the auditory system also begins looking like a single complex input element. For the very young infant there is noise or no noise, and perhaps a direction. Only with perceptual experience and maturation will this complex element be differentiated into smaller and smaller units. Again, perceptual constancy (of a voice droning on) would be innate in the single complex element, and perceptual unity (of a voice from the background noise) would be learned. Almost all noises the infant hears have strong harmonic components, and we might expect the first cell assemblies to be coordinations of the naturally occurring series of harmonics. In addition, natural sounds have rather broad bands in their frequency spectra, so early cell assemblies may also form, each of which coordinates (receives facilitation from) a number of analyzers which detect only slightly different frequencies. These first cell assemblies could form the foundation of frequency independent perception. Finally, it is in the nature of sounds (particularly those that will be used in communication) that they are very transitory (they cannot be retrieved by a scanning process) and highly modulated (their pattern of stimulation changes almost discontinuously rather than smoothly as in moving visual images). Two sound patterns in rapid succession (within the time that reverberation in an element dies out) might be coordinated by a single first order cell assembly.

Of particular interest is the coordination of the auditory and the vocal systems. From hearing himself cry, an infant may soon coordinate sound with his own vocalizations and respiratory activities. As early as the end of the first month, Piaget observes that the child begins to differentiate separate coordinations for wailing and whimpering that can be aroused separately by analogous sounds. By the third month, this differentiation has progressed further to babbling and the production of vowels and simple consonants discovered by chance as the child exercises the elements that facilitate movements of the vocal tract. These learned sounds tend to elicit imitation, especially when repeated to the child just after he has produced them himself, but the sounds the child makes are stereotyped and show no attempt to conform to differences in the vocalizations of other people. All this is typical of the behavior mediated by the first coordinations of the second stage, and we might hypothesize that the child's earliest recognition and production of a vocal sound is the result of a single cell assembly receiving facilitation from auditory inputs and kinesthetic sensations from the vocal tract, and giving facilitation to certain movements of the vocal tract and perhaps to the autonomic responses of the orienting response.

As these first vocal patterns are being formed, there are physical circumstances which guide and limit their development. First, the duration of a vocalization is limited by the requirement that the child be expiring for a sound to be produced. The process of taking a new breath may produce sensory inputs which disrupt the ongoing activities so the child can produce only a limited sequence of sounds. Even the adult speaker rarely takes a breath in the middle of a word; from the beginning there are certain limitations on the length of utterances. Second, some consonants by their nature must be produced by very transitory movements, pulses that only temporarily close a part of the vocal tract. To maintain the motor activity that produces a "k" sound would close the glottal opening and thus terminate the sound (not to mention the respiratory functions). Hence, the motor productions for many consonants must come in two steps, the first step closing the vocal tract, and the second step, perhaps facilitated by the sensory feedback from the closing of the tract, would reopen it. Even with only first order elements we can obtain chains of activity which proceed in one direction and function through sensory feedback, the feedback from the first part starting the next. Once the two elements are made active, we might expect reverberations to alternate between them and produce the familiar pairs of identical syllables so often heard from babies, "gaga," "baba," and so forth. Longer chains might be uttered, but their length is limited by the breath and the need to inhale. Finally, we should note that the earliest sounds recognized by the child are intimately related to the motor outputs that produce those sounds. Although later learning and differentiation of these early structures may produce finer discrimination, the basis for classifying similar sounds may retain a strong dependence on the method of motor production.

At about six months in the third stage, the second order elements begin to appear and are evidenced by the coordination of pairs of sounds. An example from another of Piaget's works, *Play, Dreams, and Imitation in Childhood,* Observations 9 and 10, is the case where two different sound patterns are coordinated: "pfs" and "bva." Both of these sounds are already recognized and produced by Jacqueline who, a few days before, had engaged her parents in a circular reaction, a sort of game, wherein the child and one of her parents took turns making the sound "pfs." The two sounds "pfs" and "bva" are coordinated when the child who is engaged in playing with the sound "bva" hears her father make the sound "bva;" she immediately returns to the old game of imitating "pfs," but, after a few repetitions, produces the sound "bva." Later, when she hears her father say "bva," Jacqueline says "pfs." Although the child does not produce "bva" and "pfs" together (perhaps because of breath limitations), she does have some association between the two. That Jacqueline is not merely making the sound "pfs" in response to anything her father says is evidenced by the fact that awhile later, when her father says "pfs," she says "abou" instead (a sound she had just been making which was itself derived from "bva").

When enough second order elements have been generated and differentiated perceptions and procedures formed, active experimentation begins in the fifth stage. Given a new sound, the child tries various approximations to it, usually not succeeding at first, but perservering through three or four different attempts. The child tries out several possibilities to see if one of them sounds right. This is functionally and structurally identical to the striking of an object to see if it will move in the right direction. In Observation 32a of *Play, Dreams, and Imitation,* the sound "gaga" caused the child to respond with five approximations: "mama," "aha," "baba," "vava," and "papa." Interestingly, these are almost all produced by movements of the lips, and we might imagine reverberations moving from place to place within a complex element representing lip movements while a short term memory of the two syllable structure of the sound is maintained through successive attempts. Definitely in the fifth stage are sustained attempts to reproduce adult words. Here, the order of the syllables may be established by the second syllable being facilitated by the prior production and feedback perception of the first. In addition, a second order element may coordinate the procedures for each syllable so that the reverberation of this coordinating element assures that the coordinated second syllable is used and not simply any syllable that happens also to be facilitated by the production of the first.

When a child is thinking hard and at high attention span, motor activity goes down. Again, in Observation 32a, Jacqueline tries four times to imitate a sound her father has made, but fails. On the fifth and sixth attempts she says in a whisper what her father had said (very nearly). Hearing "poupou" Jacqueline tries "bvv," "abou," "bvou," "bou," and, in a whisper, "pou" and "pou. . .ou." Since high attention span reduces activities and, in particular, motor activities; at the highest levels of attention span, we might expect a complete cessation of motor activity even though the mental processes continue. With increasing age, speech may become internalized as the gradually maturing attention span finally reaches levels that allow relatively low activity memory elements to reverberate even though the activity may not be high enough to produce a motor response.

Finally, in the sixth stage, the group of elements that mediates recognition and production of a word is coordinated by some external event to another group of perceptions and procedures which now assign the word new meaning. Before Stage Six, the only chance a child had to exercise the group of elements representing a word was in simple repetition of the word or in chance presentation of the word in adults' speech. The word was a thing unto itself and unlike the group of elements that mediate the use of a stick in reaching distant objects, the word had no connection with other activities. Now, in the sixth stage, the word becomes more reliably and predictably used by the child because of its coordination to other structures. A very simple example is the mother who touches her own nose and her baby's nose while saying the word "nose." As, in the fifth stage, the child may quickly imitate the word nose, but now the coordination to the perceptions presented (aroused) by the mother concretizes and objectifies the word; the structure representing the word "nose" now has an additional point of contact with the world, and a point of contact that may already be quite highly developed and familiar.

The Stage Six coordination of a word structure with another "meaning" structure is a higher level of development than a mere coordination of sounds with sights because the coordination is now between two complex elements, each of which has its own internal structure. An illuminating example from Observation 101 of *Play, Dreams, and Imitation* is the use of the word "bow-wow" (or its French equivalent) to indicate, first, dogs, then, later, a pattern of lines on a rug, weeks later, horses and all kinds of animals and people, and, finally, after two months of change and development, dogs and only dogs. Thus, the coordination is made to a whole group of changing, differentiating perceptions. Such a coordination cannot represent a concept because of the fluid nature of the group of perceptions the word is coordinated with. Each new differentiation or coordination of the perceptions changes the meaning and the use of the word. The way a word will be used is already implicit in whatever group(s) of procedures and perceptions it is coordinated to, but at this stage the groups that might assign meaning to a word are themselves still undergoing rapid change and refinement. If not a true concept, then at least the word and meaning coordination is a step in that direction. There is the group which generates and recognizes the word, and the group which now assigns it meaning. The word is symbolic in that it is not fully a part of the changing group of meanings, but, rather, its own internal structure (in particular its pronunciation) is relatively fixed; ultimately the word may be used independently of the meanings, just as the striking procedures may be used independently of the conditions in which they were formed; that is to say, it may be used symbolically. Through coordination with many particular structures, a given structure becomes more general, mobile, and capable of sustaining short term memory. Still, at this stage, the word is only a sign in Piaget's sense because its use, its functioning, is largely dependent on facilitations to and from the meaning group.

It is by means of the word that the social influence of language can seize hold of the internal structures and direct their development to fit social norms (in particular, the norms of language which we often express as grammar). But this is not evidenced at first; the child's first constructions of word sequences may derive from the preexisting coordinations between the groups the words are attached to, rather than from imitation of adult models. Hence, the strange ungrammatical structure (by adult standards) of the child's earliest word usage.

Only gradually will the formation of sentences come under the control of coordinations between the words themselves and become more or less removed from the groups of meanings for the words. These word to word coordinations are the start of adult grammar and their development may culminate in formal structures when the existence of the word to word coordinations are discovered (or pointed out) and themselves represented by an internal structure—perhaps a word such as "verb" or "noun." In addition, the socialization of language will, through the words, establish coordinations between the meaning groups of the words, and these coordinations will be standard for the language learned or for the community from which language is learned. Hearing two words together may simultaneously arouse the two meaning groups of those words which thus become coordinated, but which might not have been coordinated under ordinary nonlinguistic experience. Thus, the word serves as the connection between social language or grammar on the one hand, and internal images or thought processes on the other. It is to this development that we might attribute trained formal thought which develops when the coordinations between words or the coordinations between meaning groups are put under the control of yet other coordinations representing formal operations or transformations.

CHAPTER 4

OLD WINE IN THE NEW MODEL

The Structure of Learning and Memory

Learning, in terms of the model we have been developing, is simply the addition of new elements and links which themselves represent memory. The functional rules of the system naturally divide memory into three distinct levels. The first and most easily observed level is the set of elements which are currently reverberating; it is this set of most active elements which directs most of the motor activity and which determines the course of future action by directing activity into other, nonreverberating elements. The second level of memory is the set of elements which are active but not so active that they are reverberating; these elements represent a subliminal or fringe consciousness and it is from them that new reverberating elements will most easily be selected. Also, motor output elements at the second level of memory may produce motor responses of a relatively weak and automatic nature. The last level of memory is the set of elements which are not active, but which may become active if some elements having links to them begin reverberating or if appropriate sensory input activity is present; by far the greatest portion of elements of the system will, at any one moment, be at the third, inactive level of memory. The functioning of memory may be envisioned as an orderly progression of an element from an inactive state to an active state when sensory or other elements it assimilates (receives links from) are reverberating, then from an active state to a reverberating state when the element's activity ranks it among the most active elements of the system. On the downward side, the element's activity drops or is surpassed by the activity of enough other elements (or a defense response lowers the attention span) so that the first level memory element stops reverberating and is moved down into the second level of memory from where it may finally return to the bottom level of inactive elements.

Only while an element is reverberating in the first level of memory may new links be added between it and newly created elements. The kind of learning we have postulated is highly structured and exact. A newly learned item is encoded as an element that receives activity from a certain set of old elements and passes activity on to another set of old elements (the sending and receiving sets may or may not have common elements). An item is either learned or not learned at all. If later retrieval or reverberation is difficult or unpredictable, this is a matter of insufficient structure or improper retrieval. Specifically, if a newly learned item receives links from only two old elements, then its maximum activity is only two units and even this is possible only if both assimilated old elements are reverberating. Thus, the conditions for retrieval are rather precise— only a few cues will help, and all of them may be necessary. Even then, if retrieval is attempted when all reverberating elements have activities of three or more units, the elements with only two units of activity may be unretrievable. In this model, the uncertainties of retrieval are not expressed as probabilities or unexplained random events, but, rather, as a result of precise (but unobservable) structures and retrieval time conditions. If repeated use improves memory, then it is expressed as new supporting elements that coordinate the improved memory element to other elements with which it previously had no connection. A greater number of coordinations to a greater variety of other structures increases not only the maximum possible activity of an element, but also the number of different sets of cues (expressed as reverberating elements) that may bring an element to reverberation.

If learning fails to occur promptly in a new situation, as it often does for lower animals in conditioning experiments, the present model would interpret this as a structural failure and not as a subliminal increment of a newly learned item. Thus, in the statement of DS8 we note that a new element can be formed only if several elements are simultaneously reverberating, and, furthermore, only if some of these reverberating elements have links already between them. In a system with a small attention span, the chances for these conditions to be met are smaller; learning is less likely to take place and retrieval is more likely to fail.

In a rather complicated learning situation, learning may indeed proceed incrementally a bit at a time, but each step in the process is taken in an all or nothing fashion. A learning set for a particular situation is a set of elements that meets the conditions of DS8 and some of whose elements are aroused to reverberation by the learning event. In any particular experimental situation, it may be necessary for the subject to develop a learning set before the specific item being tested in the experiment can be learned. An example would be an Englishman learning associations between nonsense syllables written in Sanscrit or a cat that must learn to adopt a certain posture on hearing a certain noise to avoid shock. In both cases, the simple association or conditioned response is not all that must be learned; structures representing the perceptual events and motor events to be associated must also be built up. Even with an all or none model of learning, incremental learning must eventually show up in sufficiently complex situations. And, that each increment is itself a separate structure is evidenced in humans, at least, when a subject can remember individual trials in the learning of a single item.

When something is learned and a new element created, this new element may be created with enough links from currently reverberating elements for it to begin reverberating itself. As the new element and the old elements which it now facilitates begin to sink back into the second level of memory, we might expect their descent to be slower than their ascent because of the greater number of facilitating links added with the new element. Thus, a newly learned coordination may tend to remain in first level memory for a longer period of time than in the case of an old reverberating element that has formed no new links. This kind of functioning is observed many times by Piaget when a child discovers a new coordination (for example the doll striking coordination) and immediately proceeds to exercise or play with the new element and its supporting structures. A new discovery almost always results in prolonged activity centered about that discovery. The extra links of the new element produce a local increase in activities and the structure thus strengthened is able to maintain itself in first level memory longer than normally. But, even as the new coordination is exercised over and over, yet other coordinations and variations are discovered and learned; what was a local strengthening of the old structure is generalized and spread throughout the old structures. In the end, a certain *equilibrium* is reestablished between the parts of the old structures, and behavior ceases to be trapped at the specific point where the new discovery or coordination was made.

In an opposite situation, a newly formed element may not have enough links facilitating it to begin reverberation; an element may be created without having ever come to first level memory. This kind of implicit, unexpressed learning may occur when fairly high activity in a number of elements may prevent reverberation in a newly formed element that coordinates only a few of the first level elements. The new element stays at the second level of memory and finally drops to the level of inactivity without ever being consciously noticed or externally observed. However, in a different situation, where the activity of the reverberating elements is not so high or the attention span is larger, the same element that escaped reverberation and detection when it was formed may later be brought to reverberation.

Certainly the most remarkable feature of learning and memory is its organization and structure. The learning of new material and the retrieval of old never takes place in a vacuum, but under the strict supervision of already existing and reverberating elements. As Piaget puts it, learning takes place through the accommodation of the older schemata to the new. It is a simple and extremely important observation that learning of familiar materials is easier than learning of strange and completely new materials. In Hebb's (1949) and Piaget's (1936) models, this ease of learning new things about familiar materials is a result of already having formed the pieces out of which the new is to be formed, not as a result of subliminal associations that need only be strengthened.

Even the learning of new and strange material may best proceed by incorporating it into old familiar structures. On a very primitive level, a piece of food might be viewed as a *mnemonic device* for reliably bringing to reverberation a very familiar and well developed structure into which new perceptions and procedures may be easily incorporated. On a higher level is the example of the ancient human art of mnemotechnics which, in modern form, consists of associating (by a coordinating element) a strange new item to an old familiar one, such as a number or a place in a room. The secret of a successful association is to conjure up a specific, complex, and unusual mental image of the strange and the familiar items, for example, a visual image of the new item upside down in a pan of water in the assigned location in the room. In this way, the coordinating element has many links to and from a large assortment of old structures and even though most of the coordinated structures are irrelevant, they provide channels through which activity may be directed to the coordinating element and they provide additional elements in which short term memory may be stored. It is significant that a mnemonic image is invented while the item to be learned is in mind and the elements representing the object are reverberating. Thus, for whatever idiosyncratic reasons, the mnemonic image is constructed out of elements which are already made to reverberate by contemplation of the new item. Such an effect may be involved in learning words of a foreign language by the trick of guessing the meaning of a new word just heard, even before the real meaning is revealed. When the correct meaning is finally revealed, it is presented to a set of reverberating elements which happen to be the natural result of hearing the new word and trying to retrieve its meaning. These reverberating elements are evidence of perceptual and coordinating structures through which the sound of the new word already channels activity. These elements provide a wealth of elements and links which already satisfy the conditions of DS8, and by which the new word and its correct meaning can be coordinated.

To elaborate on the process of mnemonic invention, we might consider the presentation of a new word which has aroused perceptual and input elements to reverberation. The attempt to retrieve meaning or to invent meaning has brought to reverberation old elements that are facilitated by the reverberating perceptual and sensory elements. Without an attempt to guess or invent meaning (in this context, meaning of an element or an event is simply those elements facilitated by the element or event), the additional old elements would not have been brought to reverberation and it is tempting to hypothesize that the act of guessing or inventing involves a voluntary orienting response which allows lower activity elements to reach reverberation. Even though the additional elements brought to first level memory by a guess may represent merely phonetic similarities to familiar words and meanings, the important result is that the perceptual and motor elements representing recognition of the new word are now reverberating along with other elements which these first recognitory elements already facilitate—reverberating linked elements are required by DS8 for structural changes to be made. Finally, when the meaning of the new word is given (or when the mnemotechnic device is chosen), other elements representing this meaning (or device) presumably are aroused to reverberation. As stated in DS8, a new coordinating element is created with links from or to the recognitory perceptual elements of the word, the elements representing the correct meaning of the word (or the mnemotechnic device—a number or location in a room), and the elements representing the guessed meaning (or invented mnemonic image).

Far from being a mere trick, the mnemonic device incorporating additional old elements in the creation of a new element may be the main process by which reliable memory is constructed. Memory works best in situations where the new material itself provides mnemonic aids. It is a well known fact that logical, meaningful, organized material is easier to learn than senseless material that must be learned by rote. Meaningful material is material that brings to reverberation old familiar elements with which the new material may be coordinated. Logical and organized material is material that has parts which coordinate well with each other. Even in memorizing a seemingly random list of familiar words, organization is automatically imposed in the process of memorization. This is evidenced by the clustering of the words, on recall, into categories and groups of related words. In this situation, the mnemonic elements are taken from the items of the list. A newly learned item is represented by a new element coordinating the structure representing the item and the other structures representing the list being memorized. This new element, once formed, is pushed down into the second level of memory because of the freshly reverberating elements aroused by continued study of the other items. However, these pushed down elements are more easily brought to first level memory than completely inactive elements; the pushed down elements are still receiving activity from the reverberating structures representing the list. Short term memory may even keep some of these coordinations reverberating while new coordinations are formed. As a result, when a new item is being studied which has some connection to items already learned, the learned items may be restored to first level memory and involved in the coordination of the new item to the list structure. The connection between items on the list may be due to phonetic similarity, semantic connections (as when both words are the names of animals), or even idiosyncratic connections; in any case, the important result is that two or more items from the list are themselves coordinated through the intermediate elements that helped associate them. This provides extra mnemonic facilitations for later retrieval. Since two coordinated items link not only to the list structure but also to each other and to the common phonetic, semantic, or idiosyncratic element, such coordinated items have more facilitating links than normal. In retrieval, coordinated items may be raised to a higher level of activity and their chance of reaching first level memory is improved. And, of course, the retrieval of one of the items will tend to lead to the immediate retrieval of the other.

It would be natural to expect that the clustering effect is most pronounced when potential items of a cluster occur together in time so that the elements of one item are still reverberating as short term memory when the second item is presented. An even greater aid to clustering (and hence to learning) would be to allow the subject to arrange items into clusters on a table or scratch pad. With such an environmental clue, even inactive third level elements may be restored to first level by an examination of the clusters on the table.

An important feature of a mnemonic device is that it should be unusual or unique. Using the same image for several associations may lead to confusion on recall. In the clustering of items into categories a similar effect is found. If the cluster becomes too large it begins to break into subclusters. When a new item is being studied, and it results in the recall of a cluster from second level memory, the limits on the number of reverberating elements will prevent the entire cluster from rising into first level memory and, as a result, the new item will be coordinated only to a subportion of the cluster. In particular, the new item will be coordination to those elements in the cluster with which the new item has the most recognitory elements in common. Thus we might expect the clusters to have a certain maximum size unless they subdivide, and we might even expect the size of these clusters to vary, depending on the amount of space available in first level memory and not taken up by distracting tasks. In fact, all the above and a number of other effects concerning clustering in recall are reported or reviewed by George Mandler in his study "Organization and Memory."

Short Term Memory: Reverberations in the Data Structure

The looking-up-a-phone-number-remembering-it-dialing-it-and-forgetting-it phenomenon has led to a good deal of research concerning short term memory. Short term memory is often postulated to be a system quite different from long term memory, but in the model we are studying here, there is only one memory system which divides functionally into three different levels; reverberating, active, and inactive. We have already seen how a group of interlinked elements might maintain each other's activity at a high enough level to remain in first level memory. In addition, such a group of reverberating elements (indeed any reverberating element) passes activity on to a number of elements in the second level of memory and, in a large complex group of elements, we might envision some of the elements of a short term memory as passing back and forth between the top two levels of memory. In the following discussion, the term "long term memory element" will be used to refer to any memory element of the model and "short term memory element" will be used to refer to a reverberating element that is linked to other reverberating and mutually facilitating elements.

Each of the first two levels of memory contains not only elements that have been formed in the immediate past, but also old elements that have been reactivated and are rising up out of the third level of memory. There is an important functional difference between short term memory elements that have been recently reverberating and long term memory elements that have only begun to reverberate. A short term memory element would have links that point mostly to elements still in first level memory, and a newly reverberating long term memory element would have links that point more to elements still in third level memory. A short term memory element that moves from second level memory to first level memory would thus tend to increase the activity of the elements already in the first level of memory and perhaps provoke a defensive lowering of attention span. But when a memory element that does not facilitate already reverberating elements moves to first level memory, more activity is passed to elements in the second and third level of memory—an orienting response is made. It is interesting to note that the entry of elements of a short term memory group into the first level of memory results in a lowering of attention span and a consequent loss of elements from the top two levels of memory. In this impoverished environment, learning will proceed less efficiently and what new elements are learned will have fewer facilitating links. This is the effect of boredom (to which the infant without short term memory is relatively immune), and may account for the well established difference in effectiveness of massed and distributed learning. In massed learning, a group of elements may stay in the first level of memory and function as a short term memory depressing attention span slightly. In distributed learning, breaks between learning sessions may allow reverberations to die out so that later recall of the same group of elements now in third level memory may result in an orienting response and an expanded attention span.

Short term memory may be an important source of elements from which new elements may be generated. This is because a short term memory provides a number of linked and reverberating elements as required by DS8 for the creation of new elements. However, the effectiveness of a short term memory for this purpose is an inverted U-shaped function of time. At first, several elements to be involved in a short term memory are brought to reverberation. They are already facilitated by at least some of the elements on first level memory, but not many new coordinations are possible (having already been made). With time, activity passes through these first elements to other elements of the group in which the short term memory resides, and opportunities arise for new coordinations to form between these elements and the original elements of first level memory. Once the short term memory is established, those elements on first level memory which first aroused it may be replaced by elements that have not already been coordinated to the short term memory. The opportunities for new coordinations increase and remain high as long as different elements keep coming to the first level memory. Finally, toward the end of its life span, the short term memory may be crowded off first level memory by competing structures or by its own depressing effects on the attention span. The more often a group of elements is taken over by the reverberations of short term memory, the more connections it may develop to other structures and the more easily it may be retrieved. Thus, the effect of short term memory on learning is mixed; where it is boring in prolonged doses, in shorter but frequent doses it provides the kind of structure that is prerequisite for learning.

Since the activities of a short term memory depend on the number of reverberating elements that facilitate it, we might expect the decay of short term memory to be very sensitive to the configuration of first level memory, and not simply a function of time. When attention span is completely filled by one short term memory, the activities are quite high and may result in rehearsal or active behavioral practice which may result in the maintenance of the short term memory through circular reaction and sensory feedback. Unfortunately, prolonged rehearsal has no mnemonic value—the process of rehearsing may prevent reverberation in any but the rehearsed elements. Few or no new coordinations are formed and with the slightest distraction, rehearsed elements may be lost to the third level of memory where, having few links to elements other than themselves, they become irretrievably lost. (This phenomenon causes some embarrassment for theories of learning which postulate only associations strengthened by practice.) Another example of dependence on first level configuration is the short term memory's increased lifetime when competing structures in first level memory are inter-related, and, in general, when changes in first level memory are kept to a minimum.

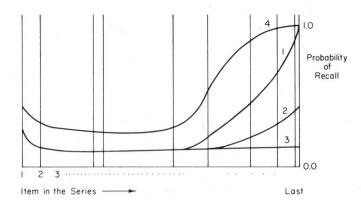

Fig. 12. Memory of a series of items presented one at a time.

In a typical short term memory experiment, a series of items is presented to the subject who is then asked to recall as many of the items as possible and in any order. The results are then presented as a plot of the probability of recall as a function of serial position. In Fig. 12, several such plots are presented together with some vertical lines to indicate where recall was perhaps possible for one particular subject (the vertical recall lines are added only to remind the reader that recall for any one word and subject is either successful or not—to obtain a smooth plot, averages must be used for many subjects or many different trails).

The trace labeled 1 in Fig. 12 is typical of the experiment where the subject is asked to recall the series immediately after presentation. There are four distinctive features to be noted. First, the final item in the series is almost always recalled as we might expect since the elements representing that item would still be reverberating as short term memory. Second, there is a sharp decrease in recall of the next to the last item, and then a more gradual decrease in recall for the last half dozen or so items. Short term memories are gradually crowded out of first level memory by the continuing presentation of new items. With many trials this decay in short term memory looks quite smooth and amenable to a mathematical description by a differential equation. However, in a particular case it is the vertical recall lines that must be explained and we might expect to find such effects as clustering and idiosyncratic mnemonics as in the case of long term recall; short term memories may have common elements and two memories with common elements might have an increased lifetime. The third feature is a long, low area of the plot where we might expect all short term memory to have decayed (to have been crowded out by more recent memories) and recall to depend entirely on long term memory elements that were added in the process of studying the items. Here recall is more difficult because it depends on having enough cues in first level memory to restore the inactive elements to reverberation. Fourth, there is a slight increase in recall for the first few items of the series; somehow there must be additional cues, more elements involved in the early coordinations; perhaps due to a larger initial attention span, perhaps because the first few items are part of the memory structure representing this particular experiment or list.

In experiments where recall is not immediately requested, the advantage of short term memory is lost and the recall probability of the last items in the series falls toward the values for the first items in the series. The trace labeled 2 illustrates this effect. There are at least two possible reasons for this boundary phenomenon. First, we might expect the middle portion of the series to be slightly depressed because of boredom and the depression of attention span by the relatively unchanging activity of attending to the items. The novel conditions at the beginning and end of the series may expand the attention span slightly and increase the possible number of facilitating links for new elements formed at that time. A second effect is cognitive: the beginning and end of the series are linked to "cognitive" elements representing the ideas of beginning and end. Thus, there is a ready cue for these elements and the subject may even remember the items as being near the ends. A brief announcement at the middle of the series that the experiment is half finished might be expected to have a similar effect although there seems to be no experiment in the literature to confirm this.

Slight novelty and reverberation in several old structures not related to the task has some mnemonic value, but if the novelty is too great or the old structures so active that they fill the attention span, then weaker short term memory elements may quickly drop to the third level and not even receive the few extra facilitations usually provided by novelty. In experiments where the subject is required to do some fairly strenuous mental exercise just after presentation of the series of items, the tail end of the plot flattens out to look like trace 3 in Fig. 12.

We might expect anything that increases the number or variety of reverberating elements would also increase the number of facilitations to newly formed elements. Thus an element formed in a "richer" first level memory or a group of new elements formed and held in first level memory for awhile would be more easily retrieved. One way of enriching first level memory may be through practice or use of a newly learned coordination. In fact, a single active rehearsal of each word in a list may result in recall with the characteristics of the trace labeled 4. Not only is the overall probability of recall increased, but the decay of short term memory is slowed. Perhaps a single active rehearsal (not prolonged, boring rehearsal) requires that a series of elements representing perceptual and motor processes must reverberate and so become coordinated to the new elements that are formed. The number of elements available to support short term memory is greater and the new coordinations are numerous and varied. As a result, short term memories last longer, and the coordinations between groups of elements that supported short term memories are more richly facilitated and more easily retrieved.

Except as noted, these effects summarized by Fig. 12 are gross simplifications of the results reported by Atkinson and Shiffrin (1967) in their study of human memory. Atkinson and Shiffrin give a theoretical analysis which is similar in some respects to the model used here but has a strong bent towards incremental and probabilistic formulations. In place of first level memory, they postulate a memory buffer with units of information that are moved in and out of the buffer by some probabilistic process. In Hebb's (1949) model, the entire data structure is a sort of buffer, and reverberations represent units of information in the buffer; the manner in which information moves in and out of this buffer is in fact determined by the links and elements of the data structure. When dealing with real data from real human subjects it is impossible to know exactly what the data structure is, and, therefore, probabilistic formulations are necessary. However, such a formulation is only an admission of what we do not and cannot know, and to proceed to the belief that a statement of our ignorance is in fact a statement of the way the brain works, is following the physicists and mathematicians too far. With sufficient knowledge of a subject's memory structures, we should be able to predict which items will be remembered and coordinated best with old familiar structures. The recall spikes in Fig. 12 must be explainable, in principle. Only in practice must we resort to the use of smooth probabilities.

Conditioning as a Form of Coordination

Conditioning experiments can be readily understood in terms of the elements of this model and the conditions favorable to the development of new coordinations. Reinforcement may be interpreted as new elements that coordinate old structures. Any event that increases the possibilities for the formation of new elements may appear to reinforce the structures that the new elements coordinate. The new elements themselves may be seen to reinforce the structures that they facilitate and, so, make them more likely to rise to first level memory. A situation or element provides, on the other hand, negative reinforcement to a structure if, in a situation that normally arouses that structure, the new element tends to channel activity away to some other competing structure.

In the case of classical conditioning, we observe the insertion of a new element coordinating a pattern of sensory input (called the conditioned stimulus), to a preexisting stimulus-response pair of elements (the unconditioned stimulus and response). In addition, the conditioned stimulus must provoke some sort of response—it must have some effect on the nervous system if only to provoke an orienting response. A structure illustrating classical conditioning is given in Fig. 13. In some situations the unconditioned stimulus and response are in fact only a reflex system, so that the coordination of this system to the conditioned stimulus is structurally a first stage development, similar to that of

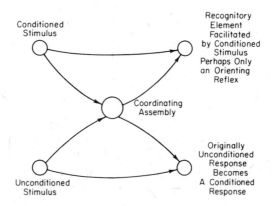

Fig. 13. Classical conditioning viewed as a coordination.

the infant. Of course, the model we have been using here immediately generalizes reflexive conditioning to cases involving mediating memory elements between sensory input and motor output; memory may act as internalized (and unobservable) stimulus and response components of a classically conditioned structure.

Perhaps the first step away from strict sensory input, motor output conditioning is the case where the unconditioned stimulus and response are in fact not an innate reflex system, but, rather, a learned structure, perhaps a perception or a procedure. Such a case may be the famous experiment by Pavlov where the placing of food in sight of a dog is used as an unconditioned stimulus to cause the dog to salivate. It is difficult to believe in an innate reflex link between visual images of horse meat in a bowl and salivation, so we might suppose the dog has developed perceptual elements that recognize the horse meat as food. That is to say, there are already first order memory elements that receive links from visual input elements and have links to the output elements that control salivation. In such a case, the unconditioned stimulus or response in Fig. 13 is in fact a memory element.

During a conditioning session, the simultaneous reverberation of the unconditioned stimulus element, the unconditioned response element, and the conditioned stimulus element will result in the insertion of a new element according to DS8. With a strict interpretation of the coordination model, we would expect classical conditioning to also require that the conditioned stimulus already facilitate some other element. Thus, a conditioned stimulus which is already familiar (that is, for which there already exist elements aroused by it) or which itself is involved in some reflex, would lead to quicker and more reliable conditioning.

Each conditioning trial should either form the coordinating element, form new elements supporting an older coordinating element, or form additional perceptual or procedural elements which might then act as the stimulus or response elements for a later coordination. Although a conditioned response may seem to be acquired gradually, it is the result of several different structural changes, and not the result of a gradual strengthening of a unitary variable. Until equilibrium is reached, each use of the new element established by classical conditioning should improve the reliability of that element by adding facilitating links and elements from other structures. This is especially the case when each trial is slightly different from the others so that additional different structures are coordinated to the original coordination. The experimental environment before the trial will itself arouse certain structures which, being active at the time of the trial, will become incorporated into the new coordination; production of a conditioned response may consequently depend on the environment in which it is attempted. The greater the variety of situations in which the conditioned response has been tried before, the less dependent on any one situation it becomes.

If the conditioned stimulus is coordinated to yet other conditioned responses, we might expect a competition effect between all the structures that the one conditioned stimulus facilitates. Unless the various responses are themselves interconnected, the original conditioned response will become less likely. In particular, the arousal of the coordinating element between stimulus and response may lead to its being coordinated itself to yet other elements if, instead of unconditioned stimulus, the environment produces some unexpected

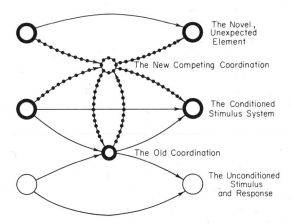

Fig. 14. Extinction as a result of competition. Heavy lined elements reverberate as a result of the extinction trial. Dotted structure is formed.

sensory feedback. Elements that have not before been coordinated to the conditioned structure may be aroused. If these elements (perhaps representing the perception of an empty food tray) begin reverberating and produce an orienting response while the old coordinating element and conditioned stimulus are still reverberating, then a new coordination may be formed. This new coordination will receive facilitation from the old structures and will therefore compete with the conditioned response for room on the attention span; extinction will result. The resulting structure is shown in Fig. 14.

There are two curious aspects of extinction. First, the rate of extinction is sometimes faster than the rate at which the conditioned response was built up. This may be because the conditioned structure itself provides a reliably aroused set of elements into which the competing structure may be immediately incorporated. On the other hand, when the conditioned response was being built up, extra perceptual elements for the conditioned stimulus may have been needed, and only slowly were extra supporting elements formed. Still, a very complicated structure with many subordinate procedures and perceptions may be very difficult to extinguish, placing each part successively under competition. The second notable aspect of extinction is that the old structure is not gone, or even changed, but merely put into competition. The old structure may spontaneously recover, especially under favorable conditions such as allowing the new (and relatively weak) competing coordinations to fall into third level inactive memory, perhaps through a long intertrial period. Or those elements that facilitate the old structure may be preactivated for the next trial (for example, showing the dish of food for a while before the next conditioned stimulus).

Generalization is readily interpreted as the arousal of the elements of the conditioned stimulus, or the coordination between it and the response, by other sensory input or memory elements. This may occur through simple assimilation of similar sensory inputs by the same element (innate generalization), or it may be a result of chaining (learned generalization). Generalization would be increased in cases where elements of the conditioned structure are facilitated by yet other structures, for example where the conditioned stimulus is already part of another system (a dog who in the past has learned to associate a whistle and light flash should easily generalize to both these stimuli even if just one is used as a conditioned stimulus). Structurally, learned generalization is similar to the Stage Four behavior of the child who uses old procedures in new situations.

A certain difficulty arises because conditioning may take place "unconsciously." However, we have already seen how new elements may be formed, but never reach reverberation before they drop into the third level of memory. Also, because the effect on the environment of an output element depends on its activity but not on reverberation, an output element in second level memory may produce motor results even though it does not reach the level of consciousness represented by reverberation. We are unaware of the details of our motor behavior. Another example might be the unconscious conditioning of an autonomic response (say the constriction of the pupil) in which a human subject is aware of the conditioned stimulus but unaware of the response and cannot normally even control the response. A lack of awareness of the response may be due to a lack of sensory feedback produced by the response.

In the case of operant or instrumental conditioning there is a third structure involved in the coordination. Not only is there a stimulus and a response, there is also a reward. When, in the presence of the stimulus, the subject makes some response, a new stimulus is presented as a reward. As diagrammed in Fig. 15, the conditioned stimulus has some internal structure, or at least provokes an orienting reflex; it is usually some recognizable feature in the environment. Also, the response in this case has no unconditioned stimulus but, rather, is given spontaneously by the subject; presumably there is a procedure and kinesthetic feedback by which the subject is aware of the response just made and by which the response may be repeated. Finally, there is the reward stimulus which usually facilitates some familiar structure and, so, on presentation results in a strong orienting response and increase in attention span

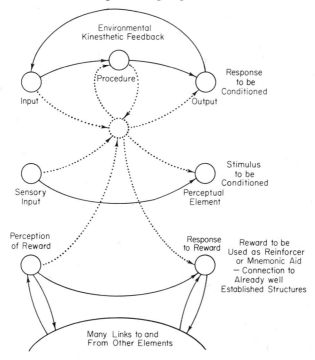

Fig. 15. Operant conditioning as coordination.

because activity passes to nonreverberating but very familiar structures. On the other hand, the intended reward may be anticipated, and may reside in first level memory so long that it produces a defense response, resulting in failure of the conditioning session. In prolonged and intensive training sessions, a dog may become overly eager for the bits of food used as reward and performance may deteriorate. The trick in operant conditioning is to get all three structures reverberating together. Often the response has to be shaped; the original coordination is with a response that the experimenter does not quite want, but, through the process of differentiation and further coordination, the response develops into a structure that produces the results sought by the experimenter. The reward is only a mnemonic device; it is usually assimilated by a well developed structure and, for the purposes of the experimenter, a structure that is easy to set into reverberation. In the development of the human infant, this concept of reward never arose; there was much more symmetry between coordinated structures. In the case of conditioning experiments, the experimenter is usually attempting to develop some innane response for which the subject would have no use or interest—that is, some response which contributes little facilitation to any of the subject's already developed structures or which has no relation to any of the subject's established circular reactions. The reward is a way of providing some arbitrary connection to an established structure.

It is a relief to find that classical and operant conditioning can both be viewed as coordination; a large number of experimental results can be immediately incorporated into the model. The chief distinction between the two kinds of conditioning models is based on how many of the stimulus response systems the experimenter has under control (two out of two for classical conditioning, and only two out of three for operant conditioning). Such a distinction is mostly an artifact of experimental design; both conditioning paradigms have many observed phenomena in common which should be reflected in the coordination model. These phenomena and their interpretation in the coordination model are as follows.

Time Proximity

The elements involved in the formation of a new element or coordination must all be simultaneously reverberating. Furthermore, there must already exist links between these reverberating elements. Through short term memory, reverberations in well developed interlinked structures may continue so that restrictions of time proximity are partly overcome.

Practice Effects and the Time Course of Learning

Up to a point, practice, especially in slightly varying circumstances, will result in the addition of parallel coordinations, each facilitated by slightly different inputs and facilitating slightly different outputs (or memory elements). With a greater variety of coordinations, the ease with which one or several may be aroused to first level memory is increased. However, as more parallel and interlinked coordinations are added, each successive trial will be more likely to arouse one of the old coordinations in which case that trial will result in no new elements, the elements having been formed. Thus, learning increases sharply at first, but then slows down later; the chance of a new coordination being formed is inversly proportional to the learning that has already taken place. This results in the top bend of the typical s-shaped learning curve. The bottom bend of the learning curve would be due to the initial unreliable arousal of the elements (perhaps yet to be formed) which are to be coordinated; once a few coordinations have been added, the elements which are themselves coordinated become easier to arouse.

Extinction and Forgetting

If an established coordination is itself coordinated to yet other structures (that are not already related to the components of the established coordination), then the originally coordinated structures become more difficult to arouse without special facilitation from a greater number of cues. The competition of several structures which receive roughly equal facilitation from the same sources will result in extinction. In a similar fashion, increasing complexity and the development of extra facilitation to competing elements may cause an element to become very difficult to retrieve, to bring to first level memory. Forgetting results.

Spontaneous Recovery

Because the old coordination does not disappear but is only challenged by competition, it may spontaneously recover, especially with extra cues to increase its activity or if rest or distraction has pushed the competing structures into third level memory. Particularly if the old coordination was well established with supporting and parallel structures, the extinction of this old structure may be very slow if long rests are allowed between trials; with both old and weaker competing structures in the third level of memory, the old, well established structure is more easily retrieved.

Schedule Effects

Competing coordinations are themselves coordinated, and if these interconnections are enhanced by a long series of extinctions and spontaneous recoveries, then extinction may become more and more difficult; the competing elements that cause it gradually become supporting elements. Failure only leads to redoubling of effort.

Shaping

Any coordination, once established may lead to differentiation in the coordinated structures and even further coordinations to other structures. Part by part, a complex structure may be developed by refining and stringing together old structures.

Generalization

Because a stimulus (or facilitating) element of a coordination may be a memory element which is itself a coordination, there may be a variety of sensory conditions that are capable of arousing it. Through chaining, a response may generalize to quite different sorts of stimuli, even in different sensory modes, or, through differentiated perceptions all facilitating the one memory element, generalization may be to small changes in stimulus. The effects of generalization might be expected both for the stimulus and the response elements of a coordination (that is, for both the elements that facilitate and the elements that are facilitated by a coordination).

Second Order and Generalized Reinforcers

Once a structure is well established or reinforced by coordinations to another easily aroused structure, then that structure may in turn coordinate to new structures and reinforce them. Also, the more complex a structure is and the more well developed structures it is coordinated to, the better reinforcer it becomes itself. And its greater structural connections make it more difficult to extinguish. Thus, a behavior that started out having to be rewarded to get it performed, ends by becoming a reward in itself.

Transfer of Training

Once a response has been made easy to arouse by coordination to some well developed structure, that response may, through chaining, be aroused by yet other structures. This transfer of training is typical of the fourth stage.

Backward Conditioning

If the stronger of two systems to be coordinated is aroused first (say, giving the dog a dish of food before giving the conditioned stimulus), it may fill out attention span with its own elements at high activities and prevent the reverberation of any elements not already facilitated by it. Otherwise, backward conditioning is possible.

Punishment, Escape and Avoidance

A reward is any stimulus that facilitates a well established (learned or innate) structure. Any structure which provides rich opportunity for reverberating elements with which coordinations may be formed is rewarding or reinforcing with respect to smaller structures it incorporates. If, on the other hand, a structure results in a paucity of reverberating elements, then it is not a good reinforcer. A structure may be relatively punishing if it has only a few elements which, once aroused to reverberation, facilitate only each other. Such a structure would not only provide small variety of reverberating elements, but it may even tend to reduce attention span since it gives little facilitation to nonreverberating elements. Lowered attention span means even fewer possibilities for learning. An extreme case of punishment is strong electric shock which arouses to high activities elements of a convulsive jerking reflex. If the reflex fails to break contact with the source of the stimulus, then the elements of this reflex operate as long as the stimulus is applied. If the electric shock has not, in the past, been coordinated to some other system, then it will now hold the reflex elements in first level memory and not facilitate any other elements. This results in a continuing depression of attention span and the first level memory becomes an impoverished environment for forming new elements. Whatever the subject does while the shock continues will be rather poorly coordinated to anything but the elements involved in the shock reflex; attention span is so reduced and the reflex elements are so active that no other elements are admitted to first level memory. But when the shock is finally terminated, the attention span may go up and whatever elements are currently in the first level (in particular the most recent motor activity which resulted in escape) will suddenly be in a rich environment for forming new coordinations. Escape or avoidance of an attention depressing situation is therefore reinforcing for whatever elements were reverberating at the moment of escape or avoidance.

Negative Reinforcement and Extinction

Extinction of escape or avoidance conditioning is difficult, and extinction of positively reinforced conditioning through punishment or negative reinforcement is also difficult. On the one hand, trials in which the punishment is not administered even for nonescape responses may not result in extinction if, in fact, extinction is due to coordination with competing structures. In normal extinction it is the arousal of the conditioned response in a new environment (configuration of first level memory) that leads to competing coordinations. But in avoidance extinction, arousal of the escape responses always results in escape, even if there is nothing to escape from. Even if the animal gives a wrong response and is not punished, no competing coordination is formed because the escape response is not even reverberating. On the other hand, extinction by punishment of a once correct response will progress slowly if the punishment lowers attention span and lessens the chances of competing coordinations, just as the extreme punishment of electric shock prevented coordinations until the escape response allowed attention span to increase. This fits with the observed uselessness of punishment for reliably extinguishing old coordinations. Punishment may temporarily depress the punished response by its effect on attention span, but the memory for the connection between the response and punishment is poor. Constant punishment is necessary to keep the response suppressed, but the closer together the punishments, the more constantly depressed attention span is, and the poorer the permanent effects on memory.

Control: States of the Attention Span

In studying a vastly complicated system it is natural and profitable to break it into many smaller and more manageable units. It is also natural, but most unprofitable, to forget in the end that the pieces are, in fact, all aspects of one thing. If the division into manageable units fails to fall along natural lines, in the end when the pieces are brought back together they don't fit like the pieces of a puzzle, but, rather, must be mixed as the colors on a painter's palette. The individuality of the original pieces is lost. While it is well to separate emotion from cognition, memory from motivation, perception from cognition, or an information processor from a decision maker; we must remember that all these aspects must finally come together to form a single, well integrated whole. Perception grades into cognition, emotional response depends on perception and cognition, motivation is towards the exercise and development of those structures already present. The purpose of this and the next section is to develop an understanding of the driving or motivational force in the cell assembly and circular reaction model.

In describing the control state of the system, the single most important parameter is the current size of the attention span. If the attention span is low and, consequently, high activity is passed on by whatever elements are in first level memory, the behavior will tend to be gross, ill-formed, and reflexive. At the lowest possible attention span there are two very contradictory reflex patterns that may function; one is sleep, a state of low muscular activity but high nervous activity, and the other is crying (at least in the infant), a state of high nervous activity with correlated high muscular activity. Which of these two reflexive circular reactions the infant will enter depends largely on the immediate past history of the nervous system. If attention span has been depressed by a continuing strong reflex action such as sucking, which involves only a limited number of muscles, then the recent activity of that reflex will, in general, have prevented other forms of motor activity, and as the reflex continues and the attention span drops, the reflex pattern of sleep is most likely since the sensory pattern of relaxation that "arouses" sleep is already present in most of the musculature. After sucking has depressed the attention span, then termination of the sucking will most likely result in sleep. But if sucking is terminated before the attention span has been depressed by the continuous sucking activity, then other postural reflexes may have sensory input patterns that are sufficiently active to reach first level memory. If, on the other hand, attention span has been depressed by continuing activity which is itself a subsystem of the crying reflex (such as gross postural thrashing, or continuing strong sensory stimulation), the reflex pattern of crying is made more likely. The inputs to the sleeping reflex might be represented by kinesthetic feedback from relaxed muscles, and the output might be represented as the central pattern of neural activity that relaxes the muscles. Viewed as a low attention span reflex, sleep must involve high neural activities and be sustained by only a few elements at a time. Sleep could be viewed as a particularly strong automatic circular reaction. Infants with low attention spans anyway, might be expected to sleep a lot. However, prolonged sleep with its accompanying relaxation of muscles may itself change the input sensitivities of the muscles and the kinesthetic feedback to the sleep reflex may fail. Also, sleep may produce metabolic changes which alter the reverberation ratio that is maintained by the system (by changing the "certain fraction" in OS5 and OS6). The depression of attention span is reduced and the sleep reflex may gradually be replaced by other reflex systems.

Perhaps the best behavioral manifestation of the size of the attention span is respiratory activity. At low attention span, as during both sleeping and crying, the respiratory movements will be strong and prolonged. The reflexive controls of respiration might be represented by two competing reflexes: one reflex with an input element whose activity increases as the breath is let out and whose output element results in a new breath being taken in, and another reflex with an input element whose activity increases as the breath is taken in and whose output elements result in relaxation of the diaphram. Thus, reverberations may pass back and forth between these two reflex systems. At low attention span, higher activity is necessary to bring either input element to reverberation; a breath must be drawn in for a longer period before the reflexive relaxation of the diaphram occurs. At high attention span, the two reflex systems replace each other more easily and shallow rapid respiration results. (The respiratory reflexes are, in fact, more complicated, but the effect of attention span on this interaction would be the same.)

Both sleeping and crying may be temporarily interrupted by increasing the attention span and so reducing the activity being produced by the elements in first level memory and reducing the activity required for an element to reach first level memory. Thus, almost any stimulation may reduce central facilitation and interrupt the ongoing reflex activity. If the interrupting stimulation can itself maintain elements in first level memory, perhaps through circular reaction, such as sucking, then it will tend to replace the former reflex pattern, especially if the interrupting reflex has a greater number of separate components that can keep a higher attention span filled (as in sucking and swallowing). With increasing age and experience, the number of memory elements increases and high activity, attention depressing reflexes may be more easily replaced by lower activity, attention filling reflex and memory systems.

It may be appropriate to make a distinction between two kinds of crying: that which is accompanied by deep respiratory activity indicative of low attention span, and that which is accompanied by light and highly variable respiratory activity indicative of high attention span. When attention span is low and central facilitation is high, it takes much stronger input activity for any one stimulus to bring input elements into first level memory. After a sleeping infant has exhaled, it takes longer, compared to the awakened state, for the input pattern that arouses reflex inhalation to reach a high enough level of activity to produce inhalation. On the other hand, an awake and alert child has a more shallow and quicker respiratory pattern which we may interpret as a result of higher attention span and increased sensitivity to low activity inputs. As the attentive child exhales, the input pattern that initiates inhalation builds up and is quicker to produce its reflex response. Thus, wailing may be a reflexive kind of crying with low attention span and high activity. It is therefore difficult to distract or interrupt a wailing infant. Whimpering may be more of a learned response that functions best with higher attention span and low activities. The whimpering child is easier to distract. With regard to the maturation of the attention span, it is interesting to note the gradual decrease with age of the time spent sleeping and wailing, and a shift of crying towards a milder better controlled pattern. Similar distinctions in vocalizations can be cited for the lower animals and the more mature human. An angry dog (and a sleeping or physically straining man) relaxes the vocal cords to produce a long low growl (or a snoring sound or a grunt). This would correspond to a low attention span and high activity. On the other hand, a frightened or joyful dog will produce a short sharp bark, indicating a high attention span and low activity that produces rapid respiratory movements and generalized tension.

In the infant, attentive, alert, high attention span behavior is typified by a quiet state of muscular activity—a compromise between strong tension and complete relaxation. Usually the infant in such a state will be found to lie quietly exercising some of the low (compared to sleeping or crying) activity reflexes such as grasping, mouthing or vacuous sucking, and visual tracking. Should any of these activities result in feedback to the reflex systems, the activity in the facilitated system will go up and that in other systems will go down. Novel, unexpected stimulation (that is, stimulation of elements not already reverberating) may produce an orienting response and an increase in attention span. Contrariwise, sensory feedback that maintains and increases activity in a functioning system may result in a defense response and a decrease in attention span. The orienting response suspends ongoing motor activity and makes likely the replacement of an old circular reaction with a new one. The defense response intensifies ongoing motor activity and makes less likely the replacement of an old circular reaction with a new one. Sensory feedback in circular reaction maintains the activity of a system, consequently reduces attention span, forces other less active systems out of first level memory, and increases the strength of whatever activities are left. If a circular reaction is varied enough, attention will not drop too greatly, but will level off where the elements involved in the circular reaction just fill out the attention span, and, perhaps, subsets of the elements move in and out of first level memory so that small orienting responses are continually produced and keep the attention span from sinking too low. The contrary effects of assimilable sensory feedback to an ongoing activity and unassimilable variations in the sensory feedback thus maintain a balance between orienting and defensive responses; attention span is kept at an optimal level for the functioning of some neural structure, given some environmental condition. If the balance slips too much toward defense responses, the circular reaction becomes boring and finally squeezes too many of its elements off by reducing attention span too far. A critical point is reached where the old circular reaction breaks down. New structures are brought to reverberation and if the old circular reaction still has some elements of attention span, then new learning is possible. Any extra coordinations change the old circular reaction so it is not so boring and so that it fills out attention span better. New learning provides additional variation and the balance is restored so that the altered structure, when reverberating, has more elements in second level memory and now provokes more orienting responses. If the balance slips too much toward orienting responses, again novel elements are brought to reverberation and coordinated to the old structure. Thereafter, what caused the orienting responses is a part of the changed structure. It is anticipated when that structure is reverberating, and, as a result, the balance is restored so that the altered structure now produces fewer orienting responses. Thus, learning tends to change any structure in such a way that there is a balance between orienting and defense responses. As Piaget would say, there is a process which maintains an equilibrium between accommodation and assimilation. Here accommodation is represented by changes in the data structure, and assimilation is represented by activities feeding into already reverberating structures.

When attention span is more mature and has a greater maximum size, a rather large reduction in span may be made without going all the way down to the level where only sleep or crying may set in. An activity that fills out attention with several coordinating elements and subsystems may be dropped when attention span is reduced; such a loss of place becomes more likely as the systems involved become more and more complex and dependent on internal coordinating elements. Thus, continued circular reaction of a complex structure may lead to enough reduction in span so that some vital coordinations are forced out of reverberation. As when sensory feedback suddenly fails, a good many more reverberating elements may suddenly stop receiving facilitation. New elements (chosen out of the many different patterns constantly being presented by the environment or available in second level memory) may come to first level memory to replace the elements lost, and if these new elements have little connection with the elements of the old structure that is dropping from first level memory, an increase in span may result. The result may be that the new elements are coordinated to the old structure. Or the old structure may be entirely replaced by the new elements and attention may turn to another circular reaction.

In general, the control state of the system can be seen to move up and down the range allowed by the maturity of the attention span, a more mature system having a greater upper limit to the span. With this movement, muscular activity and other output activity changes. From a high attention span, diffusely focused and with little motor output, the system moves to a lower attention span (with most of the reverberating elements interfacilitating or supported by sensory input) sharply focused and with greater motor output (perhaps more relaxed, or more tensed). With continuing function of the same elements and a build up of activity, attention span goes down even more, the reverberating structure perhaps fails and is replaced or supplemented by another, or more stimuli or internal elements intrude and produce an orienting response. Take, for an illustrative example, the child who, presented visually with a favorite toy, reaches for the toy. In the beginning, the child has first level memory filled by a number of independent systems, few strong enough to produce a response. Because these systems are independent and do not strongly facilitate each other, the attention span may remain at a high level. The child lies quietly exercising in alternation a number of systems, tracking objects in his visual field, gently opening and closing his hand, or perhaps sucking on his tongue. When the desirable (familiar, part of a well developed structure) toy enters the visual field, memory elements are aroused to reverberation. At first these memory elements were inactive, and their increase in activity provoked an orienting response which further helped bring them to reverberation. Since the toy is familiar and part of a well developed structure, many of these newly aroused elements facilitate each other and quickly fill out first level memory. The child's attention is riveted to the toy; all behavior is now related to the toy. The toy is followed visually and the child stops sucking his tongue or making his fist as activities drop and irrelevant structures are crowded out of first and second level memory. Among the elements now in first level memory are some that coordinate vision and reaching, the child having already learned to reach for visual images. However, high attention span and low activity passed through each link may not allow strong enough activity to develop for reaching to begin. The child is stuck with visual tracking which has reflex components directly facilitated by the sensory inputs themselves. However, attention span soon begins to fall as the interfacilitating elements build up activity, and attention is focused on the highest activity elements. Reaching, which is a well developed and interlinked structure, and a structure directly linked to the visual tracking structures, may finally commence. If the reach fails to make contact, attention span may continue to drop and focus in the closed reaching structures and the strength of the reaching activity increases—the child stretches more and more towards the toy. With continued failure, attention span may fall so low or sensory feedback may become so unfamiliar that the reaching structures are pushed out of first level memory and replaced by others. If the reach makes contact, new sensory input will arouse new elements and perhaps result in grasping. Attention span may go up, reaching may cease to function, and a new activity takes over. The child brings the toy to himself and begins playing with it, exercising his internal representations of the toy.

In normal adaptive behavior, the child oscillates rather rapidly between a diffusely focused mental control state and a more sharply focused motor control state. Reverberations concentrate in a single system until that system is lost (it became too boring) or replaced by another. Then, as relatively new elements begin receiving activity, attention span increases and motor output decreases until enough elements of one system come in, maintain themselves, and initiate new motor activity. Not only might a strongly interconnected group of elements depress attention and result in increased activity of elements, but they may also each have a link to a particular motor output element and so, by summation, produce a motor response without depressing attention span at all. Also, one group of elements with a number of coordinations and links to another group may be smoothly replaced by the other group without changes in attention span. Thus, well developed structures come to operate smoothly and without disrupting the balance of activity between first and second level memory.

The cognitive reflexes formalized in OS5 and OS6 do more than control the level of motor activity and the focus of mental activity. They also determine when new elements will be created—whenever attention span is great enough to allow several interlinked elements from more than one system to be concurrently reverberating. Creation of new elements also depends on how strongly interlinked each system is; if a system is so well interfacilitated that it can fill attention span with its elements and only its elements, then no learning will take place. (A system is well interlinked precisely because it is so well learned that all possible coordinations have already been made.) Use (reverberation) of a well learned structure involves only practice, pure assimilation, or play as Piaget says.

But, if elements from other systems that are not already linked to the reverberating system can reach first level memory, then there is a possibility that new coordinations may be formed. As the maximum attention span increases with maturity, systems that once filled the span will no longer do so, and new elements will be added. Thus, learning will tend to keep a well used system at a certain level of complexity and self-sustaining interconnection. A gradually maturing attention span sets this certain level of complexity and thereby sets a limit on learning.

A well learned, highly interconnected structure representing a sensori-motor skill may be run off at a low level of attention and corresponding high level of link activity. The structures mediating the skill come into first level memory and reside there until attention span has been narrowed down to them enough for the activity in the motor output elements to produce a motor response (which may happen even with the output elements still in second level memory). As long as sensory input supports (facilitates) it, a sensorimotor skill can remain in control of first level memory. The more complex the structure is, the longer it can stay in control and the less it will depress attention, constantly switching different elements in and out of first level memory. Also, the more complex a structure is, and the higher the attention span in which it is reverberating, the faster its associated motor actions will be run off. The most primitive example of this is the difference between high and low attention respiration. If some sensory input elements are aroused which do not facilitate those elements already in first level memory, then the ongoing activity may malfunction as some of its elements are forced out of reverberation by the competing unassimilable sensory elements. If the competing elements bring with them another set of interconnected structures, or even if they simply have links that facilitate elements not part of the already reverberating structure, an orienting response will expand attention, activity will drop, and new structures may come into first level memory and be coordinated to the old structures already there. Involving the sudden expansion of attention and the simultaneous reverberation of the unrelated old and new structure, we can see how this orienting response contributes to a rich opportunity for the addition of new elements. Together, the orienting and defense responses of OS5 and OS6 provide a balanced driving force that controls the learning process. This summarizes the main point of this section; the cognitive reflexes, OS5 and OS6, balance reverberation and activity, and, so doing, balance learning and function—accommodation and assimilation are controlled by equilibration, as Piaget states it.

A few more interpretations relating the control state may be given. The "aha" phenomenon of sudden recognition is well known. This may be a result of sudden insight or recall of a well organized memory structure and the consequent changes in attention span. Thus, the first level memory may be proceeding normally with elements of some structure passing in and out of memory when one of the new arrivals is found to have few or no links to the other elements in first level memory. Through chaining, this element has been brought to reverberation; an insight which was implicit in the old structures and their interconnection is discovered. If the newly reverberating element passes much activity to inactive elements in the third or second level of memory, then a strong orienting response is evoked and the inactive elements begin arriving in first level memory. The orienting response continues until enough of these elements are brought to reverberation to restore the reverberation ratio. The attention span having expanded along the way, not all the old structure has been lost, only its activities have perhaps decreased. The result is that a number of elements from two previously independent structures are reverberating together. New elements are now formed to coordinate them and the discovery of their latent connection is recorded as long term memory. The subjective "aha" may be a correlate of the rapid increase in attention span. (The opposite experience of boredom, depression, and letdown may be correlated with drops in the attention span.)

Finally, the changes in memory function during dreaming or hypnosis might be explained as changes in attention span that accompany them. During sleep we expect the attention span to be rather small, but during dreaming and rapid eye movement sleep the attention span may be increased somewhat so that other elements may reverberate even though the structures supporting sleep continue to function. Still, the attention span is not high enough for awakening to occur, nor for many complex structures of elements to function properly. Structures are not fully aroused; only an abnormal few of their parts reach reverberation: hence, the hazy and illogical quality of the dream. Also, any learning in this relatively depressed attention span will involve only a few facilitations, and unless the attention span is increased by awakening while these new elements are still active, they may drop to inactivity without developing the number of facilitations normal for elements formed in the awakened state. Most dream elements become impossible to retrieve.

A similar effect may be involved in hypnotic age regression or suggestability. A low attention span induced by the boring, relaxing processes of hypnosis (or perhaps by metabolic changes) would leave the adult, well structured mind unusually dependent on sensory input for reverberations (the usual processes of extended chaining being impossible). Suggestion from the outside would set up reverberations, and, once started, the short term memory of these reverberations may last for long spells without bringing additional elements to first level memory. Suggested elements would tend to stay in control of first level memory, assimilating whatever sensory input there was, maintaining whatever motor activity there was, and, in general, reducing the reactivity and autonomy of the central processes. Memories which are normally difficult to retrieve because they have few facilitating links or too much competition, may, in the hypnotic state, be recovered, especially if the right cues are placed in first level memory from the outside. Autonomic responses and otherwise subliminal elements may be brought to reverberation. Memories formed in childhood when the attention span was generally lower will have fewer facilitating links than more recent memories. Forgotten childhood skills and memories that have never before emerged into the adult consciousness may become possible to activate under hypnosis.

Drive and Motive Inferred from the Model

Because learning takes place most efficiently at the higher attention spans, we could expect behavior and environmental conditions that increase attention span to be the most strongly recorded in memory and the most clearly evidenced in behavior. In English, we would express this expectancy by saying there appears to be a drive or motive impelling the system towards states of high attention span and complex structure. There is a drive towards learning or accommodation, as Piaget might say. Any process that exists and functions automatically, implicitly contains within itself the drive that makes it go. In the model developed here, there are no drives. There are only processes. There exists the process of (and therefore a "drive" towards) accommodation—changes in the data structure of elements and links (OS8). There exists the process of (and therefore a "drive" towards) assimilation—changes or transfer of activities in the data structure (OS1). Accommodation is learning; assimilation is functioning. The formal model developed here describes these processes and the interaction or balance between them; the formal model describes the changes these processes make and the conditions under which they are made. The process of accommodation produces (causes, drives) learning, and the process of assimilation produces (causes, drives) functioning.

Assimilation and accommodation interact very strongly and intimately. In order to know the results of accommodation (as expressed by OS8) we must first know which elements are reverberating—we must first know the results of assimilation. In order to know how assimilation proceeds (as expressed by OS1) we must first know the structure of the links and elements—we must first know the results of past accommodations. While dependent on each other, assimilation and accommodation are in some respects antagonistic. The high activities in reverberating elements produced by assimilation result in lowered attention span and a decrease in accommodation. However, it is only through the functioning of the elements that circular reaction with the environment or between structures is possible, and it is only through this circular reaction that novel results are discovered and accommodated. On the other hand, the high attention span that favors accommodation results in lower activity and a decrease in assimilation or circular reaction with the environment. However, it is only through the creation of new elements that new and different possibilities for assimilation increase. Thus, moment by moment, assimilation and accommodation are antagonistic, but over the long run they contribute to each others increase. Between them the two processes of assimilation and accommodation maintain a balance; excess accommodation increases the number of memory elements and, hence, the opportunities for assimilation; excess assimilation increases the discovery of unexpected patterns of sensory input or internal reverberations and, hence, provides new opportunities for accommodation. And the fulcrum on which the balance rests is the reverberation ratio, the fraction of total activity that is to be kept in reverberating elements. The location of this fulcrum may vary with age, with metabolic changes, and perhaps with external interference, as with drugs or implanted electrodes.

Associated with every schema (associated with every structure of interconnected assemblies) there will be an accommodative and an assimilative "drive." If a structure is small and its elements strongly interlinked, for example a reflex structure that has strong feedback through the environment, then that structure will tend to capture first level memory and dominate behavior; we would say there is a need for this structure to be exercised and we might assume there is a "drive" towards the appropriate sensations. Such a "drive" is only a hypothetical construct and the effect we are trying to explain with it is only a result of the nature of the structure and its interaction with the operating system. Such a small structure is primarily assimilative. Other structures that happen to be coordinated to an assimilative structure might be described as being subordinate to the assimilative structure for the simple reason that reverberations of the other structures may quickly pass on to the attention trapping assimilative structure. And, from an external point of view, the easiest way to arouse the other structures may be through the behavior dominating assimilative structure. Therefore, we might say that the function or reverberation of the other structures is motivated by the assimilative structure.

On the other hand, if a structure is large and diffuse so that all its assemblies cannot reverberate at once, for example a memory structure representing some complex portion of the environment such as an object or a territory, then again that structure would tend to capture first level memory and dominate behavior. But, in this case, the behavior would be highly variable as reverberations passed from one part of the structure to another. There would appear to be a need to exercise this structure also, but we would explain it as a drive towards exploration or curiosity. Again, the hypothetical construct of drive is an attempt to explain what is only a result of the nature of the structure and its effect on the operating system. Such a large structure is primarily accommodative. Other, smaller structures that happen to be a part of it may undergo prolonged differentiation as they are coordinated first to one part of the accommodative structure, and then to another. Also, different situations may result in reverberations in different parts of a large accommodative structure and, so, functionally, the structure accommodates the situation. Finally, such a large structure would tend to expand attention span and result in enhanced learning; one part of the structure may induce changes in another through coordination and differentiation. Thus, a large, well developed, familiar, accommodative structure may be said to motivate (or produce) curiosity and learning of novelties or variations in its own structure. A preponderance of second level memory activity without balancing reverberations represents uncertainty—too many elements in second level memory from which too few elements can be selected for first level memory. Accommodation and the orienting response produce a "drive" towards the reduction of uncertainty.

Of course, structures are not purely accommodative or purely assimilative, but exhibit both tendencies or "drives" at different times. Whether a structure appears primarily assimilative or accommodative is dependent on the size of the attention span and is in relation to other structures that are interacting with it; the drive properties of a structure may vary from one situation to another. The reverberation ratio varies with metabolic factors and may change to produce a depression of attention span and an enhancement of assimilative properties of all schemata. With a metabolically depressed attention span, accommodative schemata may not be able to function smoothly. On the other hand, a metabolic elevation of the attention span may produce an enhancement of the accommodative properties of all schemata and make it impossible for small assimilative schemata to capture the whole of the attention span. To add a final level of control on the balance between accommodation and assimilation, it is possible that prolonged depression of the attention span may result in metabolic changes that shift the fraction of activity in reverberating elements upwards so that the attention span is enlarged. And, going the other way, prolonged high attention span behavior may result in metabolic changes that depress the attention span.

The Cognitive Reflexes

Some of the most interesting information relating to the formulation of the cognitive reflexes, OS5 and OS6, comes from the Russian work on the orienting response. Sokolov's book *Perception and the Conditioned Reflex* is perhaps the best source of this material for the English speaking reader. The experimentally observed orienting response is a complex of behavioral and physiological events that constitute a person's response to novel stimuli. The specific components that are included in any one activation of the orienting response varies tremendously, although the physiological components such as heart rate, respiratory rate, and the galvanic skin response are generally more reliable and may often appear, even when no behavioral motor response is made.

The orienting response has two kinds of components: the general and the local. The local response includes movements of the eyes, head, limbs, and body that tend to orient aroused sensory receptors towards the novel stimulus. These local responses might easily be interpreted as the specific reflex systems we have been representing by a linked input and output element. The general response includes autonomic changes in vascular tension, respiration, heart rate, pupil dilatation, and the galvanic skin response, and a general increase in the frequency of the brain waves recorded by the electroencephalograph, together with a decrease in their amplitude, and the cessation of any ongoing motor activity. Finally, the orienting response includes a generalized increase in sensitivities of the sensory receptors; for example, an orienting response to a sound, even though no motor response is produced, may result in increased sensitivity to both auditory and visual stimuli. It is particularly the changes in the EGG, in motor activity, and in the sensory sensitivity that suggests that the general response might be formalized as in OS5 as an increase in the number of reverberating elements and a decrease in the individual activities transmitted by central elements. The importance of the generalized orientation reflex to cognitive development lies in the fact that this cognitive reflex lowers activity and increases sensitivity at precisely the moment when something new might be learned. Motor activity slows down and perhaps comes to a halt when all sensory receptors are maximally oriented toward the new stimulus, and by increasing attention and lowering the activity required to reach reverberation, the generalized orientation response increases the chances that the novel stimuli will be noticed (sensory input elements brought to reverberation), recognized (facilitated memory elements brought to reverberation), and incorporated into the old structures (still reverberating) which led to their discovery.

Sokolov (1963) also identified a complex of defensive responses. The local defense reflexes include withdrawal of the overly stimulated sensory receptors, particularly the reflexive jerk of the hand away from painful stimuli. The generalized defense response was identified by a typical pattern of vascular changes that result from painful stimulation and that differ from the vascular changes produced by an orienting response. Where the orienting response included vasoconstriction in the hand and vasodilatation in the head, the defense response included vasoconstriction in both hand and head. One of the difficulties in identifying the components of the defense reflex lies in the fact that a painful stimulus is also quite often a novel stimulus, so that a defensive response is often followed by a compensating orienting response. After withdrawing our hand from a hot stove, we almost invariably follow up with an orienting response by examining our hand and investigating the stove. The common observation that a defensive reflex or a startle reflex to painful or excessively strong stimulation often intensifies motor output briefly is some justification for formalizing the defense reflex as OS6. This formulation of the generalized defense response as an exact inverse to the formulation of the generalized orienting response would lead us to expect a defense response to include a decrease in EEG frequency and an increase in amplitude. At least in the extreme case of electroconvulsive shock, it is true that the "defense" response includes high amplitude, low frequency EEG patterns. Formalizing the orienting and defense responses as in OS5 and OS6 provides a ready explanation of many of the phenomena that Sokolov reports. In what follows, OS5 and OS6 will be used as though they were an accurate statement of the central and generalized (that is to say, something at the level of the brain stem) components of the orienting and defense responses. And, in the present usage, the terms orienting or defense response will be used to mean only these central aspects, as opposed to the local orienting and defense reflexes. An interpretation of Sokolov's results follows.

The most important characteristic of the orienting response is its relationship to novelty. There are two forms of novelty, each with different effects. First there is an absolute or structural novelty which is the case when a stimulus arouses no elements of the data structure by which it can be recognized (except, of course, sensory input elements). A structurally novel stimulus is one that has never been experienced before and for which there is no memory, no well coordinated group of elements that it brings to reverberation. Naturally there would be degrees of structural novelty according to how many or how few memory elements can be aroused. An absolutely structurally novel stimulus could only be reacted to reflexively; in fact, in the adult, this may never occur—even the most novel visual image could at least be recognized as a blob of color. A second form of novelty is functional novelty which is the case when a familiar stimulus is encountered after a period of absence. With functional novelty, there is a well coordinated group of elements which are aroused to reverberation by the stimulus and by which the stimulus is recognized. But, at the time the stimulus is again encountered, none of these recognitory elements are reverberating. Where structural novelty is with respect to all three levels of memory, functional novelty is with respect only to the first reverberating level of memory. We might well expect structural and functional novelty to have different effects on the functioning of the orienting response OS5.

A stimulus that is presented for the very first time is both structurally and functionally novel. Such a stimulus might arouse various sensory assemblies, but few or no memory elements; the elements directly facilitated by the sensory input elements would be the reflexively linked motor output elements that represent the local orientation reflexes for the aroused sensory mode. We might envision the sequence of events as follows: the sensory elements are aroused by the stimulus and rise to first level memory and begin reverberating. Since these elements are not interconnected, all their links point to inactive elements and, as a result, an orienting response occurs as stated in OS5. Attention span is increased and additional elements (in this case, the reflexively linked motor output elements) are brought to reverberation while the activity in previously reverberating elements falls because of the increase in attention span.

Once an orienting response has occured, there are two important consequences as noted before. One is that the rate of learning goes up because of the increase in the number of simultaneously reverberating elements. An almost immediate coordination of the various sensory elements and reflexive orienting motor elements will occur; a new first order element is created. Coordinations may also be made to elements in other structures which happen to be reverberating at the same time. If the other structures are strong and often used, the recognition elements for the stimulus (that is, the coordination between sensory and orienting motor elements and these strong structures) are thereby reinforced or assimilated by the old structure. If the new elements are too poorly facilitated by any old structure to come to reverberation in first level memory, then their creation in second level memory may continue and intensify the orienting response until they finally come to reverberation or until additional supporting coordinations are formed. Thus, if the orienting response is fruitful and results in new learning, it is augmented. The orienting response and learning are so interrelated that it is easy to conclude with Sokolov (1963) that conditioning is impossible without an orienting response. In the formal model, however, the orienting response only greatly enhances learning.

The other important consequence of the orienting response is that the overall sensitivity increases. Because of the decrease in activities transmitted by central facilitations (by the links in the data structure), activity in reverberating elements falls; sensory and memory elements of lower activity have a better chance of competing with the old reverberating elements and getting onto first level memory. In particular, an orienting response enhances the relative importance of sensory input elements because these elements depend on external stimulation for their activity; while activity in memory elements is decreased by an orienting response, activity in sensory elements stays the same. It is observed that an orienting response to stimuli of one sensory mode will increase sensitivity in all other sensory modes. Here it may do well to stress the difference between the idea of "paying attention" and the idea of a high attention span. Paying attention to a stimulus or a sensory mode carries the connotation of concentration and narrowing distractability or attention span. Hence, paying close attention to one sensory mode, through anticipation and filling first level memory with memory structures facilitated by that mode, may actually impair the sensitivity of all sensory modes. Only the sensory mode attended to will overcome this decrease in sensitivity because of the higher activity in the anticipating memory structures. Thus, an orienting response to a stimulus is quite different from attending to a stimulus.

Once the structurally novel stimulus has evoked an orienting response, the local orienting reflexes will result in an increase in the intensity of the stimulus;

the eyes are turned towards it, the hand closes on it, the lips move towards it, the ears prick, the whole body turns. Eventually new coordinating assemblies and the increase in activity of the stimulated sensory assemblies will both contribute to a compensating "defense" response. If the stimulus is in fact structurally familiar, then the reverberations in the recognitory assemblies will also contribute to a defense response. (This is not really an accepted view of the defense response but is sometimes seen as a second component of a biphasic orienting response. See Bruner (1969), for a start.) At this point, the interaction between the two cognitive reflexes becomes quite complex; exploratory behavior ensues. The increase in sensory stimuli, if strong enough, may facilitate local defensive withdrawal reflexes. Or a small defensive lowering of span and increase in activity of already active elements may intensify the activity in local orienting reflexes which were first aroused by the stimulus. The net result is an oscillation between withdrawal and approach and a general increase in motor activity, both as static muscular tension and as movements. Almost any movement will produce a change in the characteristics of the stimulus and a reactivation of the orienting response. Indeed, the stimulus itself may be changing and constantly arousing new sensory elements not yet coordinated to the now growing structure of elements that represent the stimulus. At the extreme, a constantly changing, strange (and therefore potentially threatening) stimulus complex may even result in such a sustained and particularly strong orienting response that the high attention span and low activities result in motor paralysis—the system is transfixed by fear.

In the typical laboratory study of the orienting response to novel stimuli, the stimuli used are quite simple (a tone, a prick on the skin, turning on a light). A phenomenon carefully studied is the gradual extinction of the orienting response to a series of presentations of the same stimulus. The functional extinction or habituation of the orienting response is quite different from the structural extinction of a conditioned response. When the separate presentations of the stimulus are relatively close together (within a minute or so) we might expect both the structural and the functional novelty to disappear. Each presentation of the stimulus results in the creation of whatever coordinations are possible, and gradually (or sometimes promptly) the stimulus comes to have a central representation in the data structure of elements. As this representation (the neuronal model suggested by Sokolov) is completed, we might expect it to develop interfacilitations that help maintain its reverberations even after the stimulus is gone; short term memory of the stimulus becomes possible. If central representation of the stimulus still has reverberating elements when the stimulus is presented again, then the proportion of nonreverberating elements facilitated by the repeated sensory input will drop—some of them are already reverberating. As a result, the orienting response gradually dies out, extinguishes, or habituates.

A stimulus that is both structurally and functionally familiar (one that has an internal representation of assemblies, some of which are already reverberating) ceases to produce an orienting response. However, any change in the stimulus—intensification, weakening, or change in quality—produces the orienting response again. Presumably such changes arouse some different sensory assemblies that have not yet been coordinated to the internal representation, or arouse some parts of the internal representation in which reverberations have ceased. Or, if the stimulus has been continuous, when it stops, an orienting response may result; the fall in activity of the reverberating assemblies it had been supporting will alter the balance between reverberation and activity. Even a change in the length of separate presentations or a change in the interval between presentations will evoke an orienting response at the point where the stimulus was expected and did not appear, or at the point where the stimulus was not expected but did appear. This strongly suggests that even a simple stimulus such as a tone of fixed duration has an internal representation of some complexity: perhaps a chain of coordinations, each facilitating the next to represent a time interval. Even a constant sensory stimulation may, as time passes, arouse a sequence of different sensory inputs because of adaptation reflexes and changes in the sensory receptors, as when the eye accommodates to a bright light.

Once a novel stimulus has become functionally (and necessarily structurally) familiar, it ceases to produce an orienting response. However, it would be a mistake to assume that the stimulus is no longer noticed; indeed, specific adaptation reflexes (such as pupil changes to a light) continue, and if conditioning is being established, it is only with the habituation of the orienting response that the conditioned response becomes well established. The coordinating elements that connect the internal representation of the stimulus to the conditioned response, may be reverberating as part of the short term memory of the stimulus. When the stimulus arrives, it facilitates already reverberating elements and produces no orienting response. However, it increases the portion of activity in reverberating elements and may even produce a defense response. Attention span is reduced and activities transmitted by the links goes up. Being well connected, the short term memory of the stimulus is likely to stay in first level memory even after the attention span goes down; through the coordinating element increased activity is passed to the conditioned response structure. Even with habituation to nonsignal stimuli (that is, ones that have no coordination with a response to be given), such as the loud clicking of a clock, awareness is maintained somewhere in the nervous system because the cessation of the stimulus and drop in facilitation of reverberating elements produces an orienting response. While we behaviorally ignore a ticking clock, it nevertheless holds a position somewhere near the lower end of our attention.

In general, the orienting response to an habituated or "ignored" stimulus can be restored in any of three ways. The first, mentioned before, is to change slightly the stimulus, thus arousing new elements that do not facilitate the residual reverberations in the familiar structure. A second way is to present some unrelated stimulus that will compete with the residual reverberations and force them off the first level of memory; such inactivation renews the functional novelty of the older stimulus and, when the old stimulus is presented again, there are no reverberating elements which it facilitates, and an orienting response is again evoked. A third way of restoring the orienting response is simply to wait long enough for the reverberations in short term memory to die out or to be replaced by the driftings and meanderings of the mind.

It is interesting to note that the last two methods of restoring the orienting response result in a rather stronger orienting response. An orienting response to a structurally familiar but functionally novel stimulus is generally stronger than the orienting response to an equally strong stimulus that happens to be both structurally and functionally novel. Familiarity produces a stronger initial orienting response, but one that habituates more easily. We might attribute this to the fact that a structurally familiar stimulus arouses a greater number of inactive memory elements; it upsets the balance between reverberation and activity more than the unfamiliar stimulus which arouses only sensory elements. Also, with familiar stimuli, the first few elements brought to first level may have many links to other yet inactive elements; this would continue or increase the orienting response. That the orienting response to a structurally familiar stimulus is rather quick to extinguish may be because only one brief presentation of the stimulus is enough to reliably arouse the entire structure which, if well developed, may maintain its reverberations for some time. In contrast, the structurally novel stimulus produces an orienting response that cannot be extinguished until an internal representation for the stimulus has been built up; and how long that may take depends on the complexity and intensity of the new stimulus.

Once learning has taken place and the stimulus has become structurally familiar, a number of changes take place in the reaction to that stimulus when it is presented later as a functionally novel stimulus. We have already noted the stronger but more easily habituated orienting response it produces. If the stimulus has been given signal value by coordination to some response structure, then the range of stimulus intensities that can produce an orienting response increases. Both milder stimuli that were not noticed before (as evidenced by an orienting response), and stronger stimuli that produced a defense response before, will, given signal value, produce only the orienting response. Coordination to response structures results in a larger internal representation of a stimulus; weaker stimuli can cause a stronger unbalancing of the reverberation ratio, and stronger stimuli may be drained off into response structures so that reverberation does not become too great without compensating increases in activity in the second and third levels of memory.

Another example of the effect of learning on the orienting response is provided by the case where the subject has been given instructions to perform some motor action in response to one stimulus and not to another similar stimulus. The motor response is already familiar and presumably represented by previously learned structures. The problem is to coordinate one stimulus to the structure that represents the motor activity and the other stimulus to the structure that represents withholding the motor activity. However, the subject doesn't know in advance which will be which. In such a situation, the stimuli are given signal value, and Sokolov reports several interesting changes in the orienting response. First of all, giving the instructions probably results in activation and reverberation of parts of the old stimulus and response structures mentioned in the instructions. In fact, giving the instructions results in a strong orienting response and a lasting fall in skin resistance and rise in EEG frequency. Second, the orienting response to the stimuli to be discriminated is intensified; from the instructions, they were partly anticipated and were to some degree familiar. While the exact pattern of sensory stimulation was not known (a high pitched tone or a low one), the sensory mode involved is known. Anticipation of some sound, for instance, would bring perceptual elements related to auditory recognition to readiness. In effect there is both structural familiarity, that the stimulus will be tones and will be coordinated to certain responses is known, and functional novelty, exactly which structures will be used and what sensory input patterns will occur is unknown. As in the case of purely perceptual learning, structural familiarity and functional novelty produce a stronger orienting reaction. Interestingly, the more difficult the discrimination (the more alike the two stimuli being used) the larger the orienting response becomes. A finer discrimination would require a higher attention span that admits to reverberation the lower the activity assemblies that represent the small difference between the two stimuli. Finally, we should note that the competition between the two similar but yet different structures produces a resistance to habituation of the orienting response—uncertainty produces a continuing functional novelty.

Although most research on the orienting response has a strong bias towards the perception of stimuli and the learning of conditioned responses, the formal model of cell assemblies assumes that all elements of the data structure—sensory, motor, and mediating memory elements— have the same functional characteristics (almost). We should therefore expect the generalized orienting response to have an important role in strictly cognitive functioning. Charlesworth has pointed out the relation between the orienting response and the cognitive "emotion" of surprise. What distinguishes surprise from the usual orienting response to novel stimuli is an expectation produced by internal cognitive structures which is contradicted by sensory inputs or by other cognitive structures. In the cell assembly model, such an expectation would be represented as activity and reverberation in an old group of interfacilitating elements. Such a group of elements is normally active only during a circular reaction with appropriate environmental events, and the smooth movement of elements in and out of first level memory depends on appropriate sensory support from the environment. At all points where past experience had aroused elements not already coordinated to the group, we may presume that new coordinations were promptly formed. As a result, all elements that have been coordinated to other members of the group may, to some extent, be anticipated; even without sensory stimulation other members of the group may pass activity to the anticipated element and raise it to first level memory. Confirmation of the anticipated assembly may occur when the additional activity from sensory input finally arrives and increases the activity in the already reverberating element, and, as discussed before, results in motor response (or, perhaps, only an internal response and passage of reverberation to other memory structures). However, in the case of surprise, the confirmatory stimulus never arrives. Instead, some other unanticipated stimulus arrives and sends activity to elements not in first level memory; the result is an orienting response. The mere absence of confirmatory stimulation, even without contradictory and surprising stimulation, may result in failure of reverberations in the anticipated structures; again, the result is an orienting response. Also, the absence of one stimulus is often a different stimulus; darkness, the absence of light, in fact produces sensory stimulation.

Going a step still further into the cognitive domain, we might replace the unanticipated sensory input with unanticipated activity from other internal structures. In such a case, a single element may have been at one time coordinated with one group of elements, and at another time with a different group of elements. Subsequently, reverberations in one of these groups may pass activity through the common element to the other group and result in the unexpected arousal of enough elements of the other group to produce an orienting response. Both surprise reactions, cognitive-stimulus and cognitive-cognitive, could play very improtant roles in cognitive development. Cognitive-stimulus surprise may play a key role in the development of conservation— Piaget's (1941) term for learning to coordiante a variety of different sensory perceptions into a single group so that all the different perceptions can be viewed as one thing and responded to accordingly. And cognitive-cognitive surprise might play a key role in the later development of formal operations— Piaget's term for learning to group and coordinate different sensorimotor structures so that the learned groups and coordinations can be used independently of specific sensorimotor activity.

The important result of a surprise reaction is, suffer its being said yet again, an increase in the size of the attention span and an enhancement of the learning process. There are at least two requirements for optimal learning to take place. First, the attention span must be sufficiently large to admit a number of elements both from the old reverberating structures and from the unanticipated structure to first level memory. For a newborn infant whose maximal attention span is quite low, learning may proceed no faster than a single coordination of stimulated sensory inputs and reflexively activated outputs at a time. Only for the adolescent is the rapid coordination, all at once, of mediating memory elements from several different structures possible. A second requirement for optimal learning is that the old structure and the unanticipated structure must be capable of reverberating together. Such functional simultaneity might be supported or caused by elements the two structures happen to have in common, by simultaneous sensory stimulation of both structures, by motor outputs of one structure resulting in sensory inputs to the other structure, and, in the case of cognitive–cognitive surprise, by chains of coordinations of the two structures through other structures. If the attention span is not large enough to hold both structures, then orienting responses may continue until both structures have been brought into first level memory and the reverberation–activity ratio is restored. Otherwise, there may not be enough unanticipated elements brought to reverberation for retrievable coordinations to be formed; or, through competition, enough elements from the anticipated structure may drop from reverberation so that its function fails and is quickly replaced by the unanticipated structure without much time for coordinations to be formed. Here is the case of a little learning blocking further learning; if the anticipated and the unanticipated are in fact partly coordinated already, then reverberations may smoothly pass from one to the other without evoking an orienting response and thus missing the chance for improving the coordination between the two and working out their implicit interrelationships. Only in the case where span is large enough for both structures to function together, and, more particularly, for uncoordinated parts of each structure to function together, will learning occur. The importance of the orienting response, which causes more widespread reverberations than normal, can hardly be over emphasized; without it functioning would always run smoothly on, or else become confused and start blindly over. And the higher the attention span can be pushed beyond its normally functioning size, the more reserve there is, and the faster learning can proceed. Intelligence quotient would be a measure of this reserve rather than a measure of its absolute or normal size.

While the defense response has not been as well studied as the orienting response, Sokolov (1963) does present data which is consistent with the assumption made here that the two responses are reciprocal. Perhaps the most important contrast between the orienting and defense responses is that the defense response is very difficult and often impossible to extinguish or habituate. Where repeated presentation of a mild stimulus results in a neural anticipation of the stimulus and extinction of the orienting response, if the stimulus is strong enough to produce a defense response, anticipation can only serve to increase the defense response. According to the formalization OS5, an orienting response is possible only when activity in nonreverberating elements increases in proportion to activity in reverberating elements; therefore, a stimulus that facilitates an already reverberating structure cannot produce an orienting response. However, according to the formalization OS6, a defense response is possible only when activity in reverberating elements increases in proportion to the activity in nonreverberating elements; therefore, a stimulus that facilitates an already reverberating structure can only increase the possibility of a defense response. Even stimuli that originally produced an orienting response may, with repeated presentation, finally produce a defense response when enough elements have been built up for short term memory. Then the summation of the activity added by a repeated stimulation and the activity still in the reverberating short term memory may produce a defense response. Continued, low level stimulation without variation becomes irritating and is avoided. Thus, the repetitions that extinguish the orienting response lead to the intensification of the defense response, or even to the establishment of a defense response where one did not exist before.

A related phenomenon reported by Sokolov is over-extinction. Repeated presentation of a stimulus leads to extinction of the orienting response, but if the presentations of the stimulus are continued far beyond the point of extinction, two things may occur. One is that the subject tends to become drowsy, an indication of low attention span and high activity in the sleep complex of muscle relaxing reflexes. This is especially likely when the subject is sitting quietly in the laboratory stiuation. Also, from common experience, we know that repeated, boring presentation of a stimulus may lead to irritation, motor activity, and withdrawal (or even aggression)—again, an indication of low attention span and high activity, this time in muscle tensing reflexes. (Sleepy people are often irritable people anyway.) Either case may result from gradual lowering of attention span by small defense responses to each build-up of activity in the short term memory structures. The final result of this gradual lowering (sleep or aggression) would depend largely on the structure of the short term memory itself and which motor systems it was coordinated to.

The second thing that may occur after long over-extinction is a sudden and spontaneous (not attributable to external changes) dehabituation (disinhibition is the more usual term, but it carries connotations that are distracting here) of the orienting response to the repeated stimulus. The stimulus suddenly begins producing a response again. A most interesting fact about this dehabituated "orienting" response is its frequent similarity to the defense response, both in vascular components and in its resistance to rehabituation. Again it is as if continued stimulation of the same structure has resulted in a build-up of activity and gradual defense lowering of attention span. Dehabituation often occurs just as the subject becomes drowsy and continues while the subject is drowsy. As attention span narrows down, some elements of the short term memory may be pushed into second level memory where they are maintained at fairly high activity by the rest of the short term memory still reverberating. Then, the stimulus may give enough extra activity to these second level elements to restore them to first level. At low attention span, activities passed by each link are relatively large; for a relatively small input activity, more interlinked elements are put into reverberation and there is a disproportionately large increase in reverberation. The result is a defense response which might be identified as a dehabituated orienting response. On the other hand, the increase in activity of second level elements may produce a geniune orienting response if some of the second level elements have such low activities that they cannot reach first level even with the additional activity given by the stimulus. As long as the orienting response fails to bring more of the short term memory structure to first level, there can be no habituation. Thus, when attention span becomes so small that the short term memory begins to fail, repeated stimulation may produce mixed orienting and defense responses depending on how much of the short term memory has died out. And these defense responses are much more pronounced and observable at low attention span than at high attention span; bringing a few more elements to a small first level memory has much greater effect on the balance between reverberation and activity than bringing the same number of elements to a high attention span, large first level memory.

Sokolov has observed that a novel stimulus that produces an orienting response of its own, will also reestablish the habituation of the orienting response to an old stimulus that had become dehabituated. The novel stimulus might produce an increase in attention span that was large enough to allow the short term memory to reestablish itself. Of course, at high attention spans with low activity passed by the memory links, the novel stimulus (whose activities are unaffected by changes in attention span) would be more likely to bring its own elements to reverberation. However, at low attention span, the short term memory has relatively high activities and overpowers the activities of the sensory input elements; instead of the novel stimulus bringing its own elements to reverberation, it only produces an orienting response so that the elements of short term memory that have fallen to the upper levels of second level memory are brought to reverberation. More generally, low attention span and defense responses result in domination of the thought process by internal links and elements; high attention span and orienting responses result in greater sensitivity to and domination by stimulations from the environment. When we sleep, run, or talk aloud, we are less sensitive to external stimulation, say, someone else talking.

Other reciprocal relations exist between the orienting and defense responses. For instance, what dehabituates the orienting response may extinguish or habituate the defense response. In a series of painful stimulations which are producing a defense reaction, the presentation of a novel stimulus may result in an orienting response. It is of significance that under these conditions of depressed attention span and high residual activities from the continuing series of painful stimulation, it takes a relatively stronger novel stimulus to produce an orienting response; as discussed before, sensitivity to stimulation is lowered at low attention spans. In any event, if an orienting response is produced by the novel stimulus, then the continuation of the series of painful stimulations reveals that these stimulations may now produce an orienting response; the defense response has been replaced and does not return until several repetitions of the pain stimulus. The increase in attention span and the lowering of activities by the orienting response results in lowered activity in the reverberating short term memory of the painful stimulus; it may take several repetitions of the painful stimulus before activities in the short term memory of it are high enough to produce a defense response again. Also, as discussed before, the defense response is less pronounced at the higher attention span produced by the orienting response to the novel stimulation. Finally, if the novel stimulus is strong enough, it may compete with the old reverberations and force some elements out of first level memory; as a result, the next presentation of the painful stimulus may even produce an orienting response. The orienting response evoked by the novel stimulation has generalized to the painful stimulation. On the other hand, if the novel stimulation was not strong enough, the defense response may generalize to the novel stimulation which usually would have produced an orienting response. Again, as discussed before, novel stimulation may result in a small orienting response that only restores some of the short term memory of the painful stimulation; a strong rebound defense response results.

Many of the components of the orienting and defense responses are of a transitory nature. As an example, the galvanic skin reaction as a component of the orienting response may be observed as a decrease in skin resistance followed by a prompt return to a base level that is now slightly higher than before the orienting response. In a series of orienting responses to a repeating stimulus, the drops in the skin resistance extinguish along with the other components of the orienting response (although at different rates). As the drops in skin resistance disappear, the base level of resistance gradually rises towards the higher levels observed during sleep. It is tempting to speculate that this is but one aspect of a more general phenomenon; phasic changes made by the cognitive reflexes result in a delayed tonic change in the opposite direction, perhaps mediated by chemical or metabolic changes. As suggested before, these tonic changes might take the form of changes in the balance of reverberation and activity that controls the orienting and defense responses, the fractions mentioned in OS5 and OS6. On the grandest scale, it is well known that sleep or a period of moderate physical activity may result in a state of heightened alertness; in reverse, periods of alertness and tension may result in a state of exhaustion and sleep, or even in a spell of muscular activity to "work it off." And, on a smaller scale, orienting responses are often short lived and followed by a mild rebound defense response; interrupted motor activity is soon resumed, or new motor activity is initiated. At the other end, a defense response is also short lived and often followed by alerting and orienting towards the source of stimulation.

Pain (in the most general sense, as stimulations that are avoided either by withdrawal, by aggression, or by sleep) is any stimulation (or thought) that is excessively strong, familiar, or monotonous. Therefore, this rather long and tedious interpretation of Sokolov's (1963) observations in terms of the formalized cognitive reflexes OS5 and OS6 had best come to an end. The importance of the cognitive reflexes in regulating the process of learning demands some justification for the way they have been stated; this section is intended to provide such justification by way of saying, "Look how well it can all fit together!"

The Underlying Reality: the Brain and its Function

The brain is fantastically complex and difficult to understand. Any theory of its function is likely to provide more amusement to neurophysiologists than illumination. However, correlating some of the features of the formal model to the gross anatomy and functional characteristics of the brain may provide some additional intuitive, concrete, inductive understanding of the formal model.

To begin with, the cell assembly (the neurophysical correlate of the element of the model) is probably widely distributed in the brain and includes cells in all levels of the cerebrum and thalamus. Cell assemblies that are perceptual, and specifically sensory assemblies, would include cells in the peripheral nervous system which are directly exposed to environmental influence. And cell assemblies that are procedural, and particularly the primitive motor output elements, would include cells in the spinal cord that control muscular contraction and relaxation. Purely memory assemblies would consist of cells predominately from the cerebrum, and purely input-output assemblies would consist of cells predominately from the peripheral nervous system, the thalamus, cerebellum, and lower brain stem, but also from the cerebral cortex (the sensorimotor areas in particular). The primitive elements of the formal model are, in Hebb's (1949) neural model, large and diffuse structures of neurons that cover the entire nervous system.

Because of the nature of the interconnections of the various parts of the cerebral cortex, even purely memory assemblies must include cells in the paleocortex (including, for purposes of this discussion, the basal ganglia, the hippocampus, the amygdala, and, generally, any part of the cerebrum other than the outermost neocortex) and the thalamus. This is because the various parts of

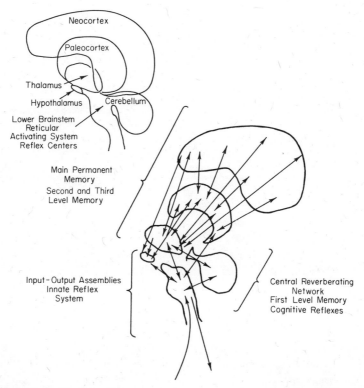

Fig. 16. Some of the major structural and functional subdivisions of the brain. Each cell assembly is spread diffusely through the nervous system and the interaction of the major divisions provides a control system superimposed on the assemblies which are in turn imbedded in the subdivisions.

the neocortex are interconnected by fibers that run down and synapse on cells in the lower structures of the paleocortex and thalamus; fibers from these cells then reach up to other regions of the neocortex. Widely separated parts of the neocortex are rarely directly connected (see Fig. 16).

Thus, the thalamus, and, to some extent, the cerebellum and the paleocortex, represents the Grand Central Station of the nervous system. Only if activity in parts of a diffuse assembly are strong enough to arouse the cells of that assembly that are in the thalamus, cerebellum, or paleocortex, will the activity of that assembly be spread to all its cells in all the various regions of the nervous system. Only when a pattern of activity succeeds in impressing itself on these central structures will it begin to reverberate. These central structures form a sort of major data register in which all first level memory must at least in part reside; they would seem to define what is on attention in the formal model. Given some patterns of activity coming into the central brain structures, they are rebroadcast as patterns of activity back to the other structures of the nervous system. Thus the reverberation of a cell assembly might be viewed as an internal circular reaction between the central register (the thalamus and related structures) and the peripheral register (the peripheral nervous system, reflex centers, and ganglia), or perhaps the memory registers (the neocortex). The existence of a link from one assembly to another is merely a formal statement of the presumed neurological fact that, given that the first assembly is reverberating, the pattern of excitation and inhibition being broadcast by the central register not only maintains the activity of the first assembly, but also passes activity on to the cells of the second assembly.

The neurons of the central register are themselves interconnected. As a result, the pattern of activity broadcast to the rest of the nervous system when two assemblies are reverberating is different from a simple combination of the two patterns that would be broadcast for each separately. The activity of each of the reverberating assemblies induces small changes in the activity of the other; both assemblies must function through the central register where the more or less random interconnection of the cells they happen to use produces extra facilitation of some cells and inhibition of others. Therefore, what is broadcast is largely a simple combination of the two patterns broadcast for each separately, plus a pattern of activity that represents the interference between the two old patterns. This new interference pattern is largely a product of the idiosyncratic connections between the neurons of the central register; in this sense, the central register has produced, in the interference pattern, a randomized code representing the conjunction of activity in the two assemblies. This randomized code might be incorporated into the brain by the formation of a new cell assembly with its own pattern of activity, the central register part of which is the interference pattern. The new assembly, being formed while certain old assemblies are reverberating, will include cells from the old assemblies. These cells are combined with new cells recruited by the interference pattern to produce a distinct new cell assembly. This new assembly includes cells from the old assemblies and, therefore, represents a copy in miniature of the old assemblies and their link relationships. Thus, at the neural level, the formalized rule DS8 for the addition of elements states: when activities in several different assemblies are strong enough for the assemblies to be passing activity through the central register to other assemblies that are also passing activity through the central register, then some cells from each of the involved assemblies, from the central register, and extra cells aroused by the interference pattern, are formed into a new cell assembly. The process by which the new cell assemblies are formed is presumably that described by Hebb. Finally, it should be admitted that the central register is highly structured and the "randomized" code is not entirely random. In the formal model this innate structure is supposed to be represented by the innate reflex links of the data structure.

The attention span is not constant and, also, the reactivity of the central register is not constant. The relative strength of sensory input activities and the link activities of the memory assemblies varies with the reactivity of the central register. In the brain, control of attention span and central link activity may be provided by the reticular activating system of the lower brain stem. Although the situation is confused, it seems that the lower brain stem has ideal connections for the location of the cognitive reflexes. It is in a situation where it can moniter the total reverberations of the central register, where it can control the reactivity of the central register, and where it can control the reflex centers for the autonomic responses often associated with the cognitive reflexes. Further, it has strong influence on the lower reflex centers and can perhaps alter their reactivity inversely to the reactivity of the central register structures. Finally, one element is missing; the lower brain stem is in a poor position for monitoring the total activity in the upper reaches on the neocortex. How could it maintain a balance between reverberation and activity? The paleocortex is in an ideal position for this function; it stands between the thalamus and the neocortex to some extent. The existence of connections between the upper reaches of the reticular activating system and the amygdala and other parts of the paleocortex strongly suggest that the control of the cognitive reflexes is shared between the paleocortex and brain stem. The frequent experimental evidence for involvement of parts of the paleocortex in emotion, short term memory, and motor control (all aspects of variations in attention span according to the formal model) suggests its importance for the control of attention span and paleocortex. It is certainly involved in long term metabolic regulation.

Finally, a structure that is intimately involved in the control of the metabolism of the entire body is the hypothalamus. This structure also receives connections from the cerebrum and thalamus, and has a very profound effect on the reactivity of the entire system. It is possible that the hypothalamus controls the setting of the reverberation ratio that is then maintained by the brain stem and paleocortex.

But a million other things are also possible, so I will stop this speculation here. The interested but uninformed reader is referred to Thompson's excellent introductory text to see why. The only point to be made here is that the formal model does relate sensibly to what is known about the brain's structure and function. In brain studies, sure proof or prediction is almost impossible. I offer up this section only to give additional concrete images of the formal model. The child can only begin to appreciate the nature of his rattle after he has coordinated the sight, feel, and sound of it. So, here, a neurological discussion is added to give another perspective on the formal model and, so, objectify the reality behind the model by connections with a number of already accepted realities.

CHAPTER 5

ELABORATIONS AND SPECULATIONS

The Assembly and its Meaning

An assembly or element of the data structure is the internal representation of an event in the environment. An event in the environment can only be detected as the input sensations and assemblies it arouses, and as the motor activities and assemblies that can give further feedback of more sensations and active assemblies while the event is occurring. Eventually, this internalized representation of an event can become so complex that it may become active even when the event is not occurring. The output activities of the representation may in fact cause the event (or, rather, a recurrence of the event) to occur in the environment. This independence of the internal representations from sensori-motor control and subordination of the environment to internal changes has its earliest beginnings with the chaining behavior observed in Stage Three. This independence and subordination is perhaps the very essence of intelligence—the seeming ghost in the machine.

An element in the internal representation is the coordination of whatever elements have already been created and are aroused by the external event represented by the element. Given reverberations in some of the old elements as

133

cues, the new coordination can arouse the rest of the old elements as retrieved information; the coordination tends to recreate the pattern of reverberations that caused it to be formed. Here is the old Gestalt principle of completion.

For any new event in the environment, only those aspects of it that have already been experienced and encoded in earlier elements can now be coordinated as representations of the new event. This new coordination represents two things: first, a conjunction of all the elements it coordinates, of all the aspects of the external event to which the internal structures respond by reverberating; and, second, a relation between these aspects; some of the aspects arouse the new coordination and are precursors to the new event, and the rest are aroused by the new coordination and follow from the new event. As illustrated in Fig. 17, an event in the environment (or even an imaginary event which exists only as a representation in the mind) will arouse certain pairs of elements which already have a relation, and the new coordination represents the conjunction of all these elements and their relations. Of course, later addition of elements may change the original meaning of this new element just as the new element changes the meaning of the old elements it coordinates. The hypothetical event of Fig. 17 arouses all the elements shown on the left, and this event is encoded as the new element and links in dotted outline on the right. The process of coordination formalized by DS8 does not simply make all possible associations, but only the more active, more important ones (as a result of OS2), and even then only forms new connections in certain places and in certain directions depending on the old data structure.

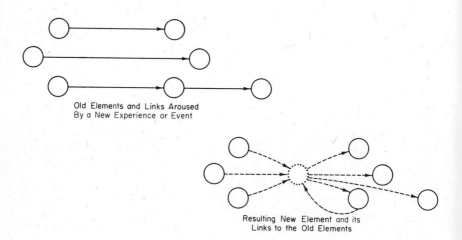

Old Elements and Links Aroused
By a New Experience or Event

Resulting New Element and its
Links to the Old Elements

Fig. 17. The meaning of an element.

The meaning of a specific element or group of elements is the set of elements that facilitate or are facilitated by the specific element or group, and nothing more. These facilitations may come from sensory inputs or they may come from other memory elements; they in turn facilitate motor or autonomic outputs or they may facilitate other memory elements. Usually we think of meaning as having some external reality, and indeed we might trace the facilitations of an element through several layers of mediating elements back to input and output elements which are in turn "linked" to the environment and external meaning of the element. But defining meaning by the immediate connections of an element, we gain a certain simplicity; it is difficult enough knowing what the "meaning" of an element is without having to also know the "meaning" of that part of the external universe which it represents. For meaning, the nervous system is self-referencing; it's just that some of its elements are exposed to external meddling, and, in turn, some of its elements just happen to meddle with the environment.

It may be useful to distinguish between the facilitating elements and the facilitated elements of any one element or structure as the cued meaning and the retrieved meaning respectively. Given the cued meaning as reverberating elements in first level memory, the formalization of attention span, OS2, assures that only the most meaningful elements are retrieved and brought to reverberation. Also, the orienting and defense responses formulated in OS5 and OS6 regulate the amount of cued meaning that is necessary for retrieval, and the amount of retrieved meaning that will result. Finally, there might be a distinction between the entire structural meaning of an element and the functional meaning which is the subportion of the structural meaning which actually reverberates.

An element can be viewed in two ways: as a processor or transformation of internal activities, and as a structure or representation of external realities. Where the links only transfer some unit of activity from one point to the next, an element can collect and disperse activity. Also, the element will perform its transformation of activity only if its collected activity is sufficiently high. Thus, while the elements act as processors and decide the flow of activity, there is another layer of control, the attention span and the orienting and defense responses, which in turn decide how many elements will share control of the flow of activity. Finally, the system closes on itself because the attention span, the second layer of control, in turn depends on the reverberation ratio which is a function of the activities of the elements, the first level of control.

As for representation, the internal structures of first and higher order elements are the equivalent of mental images, a stronger more detailed image being a more complex structure of well interlinked elements. A more concrete image would be one with more links from and to the input-output elements. As these mental images or structures become coordinated with more and more third order elements, they become more internalized and can function (carry out their transformations of activity) without observable external behavior. The third order elements will add two things to these groups of elements. First, they will serve to bind the groups into more strongly linked structures, and they will allow faster movement of activity with a structure from any one element to another. Second, these elements are entirely facilitated by other memory elements and they facilitate only other memory elements; they are more removed from external sensory control and thus they become symbolic.

The earliest coordinations formed very small systems of representation, so that an element, once active, tended to keep itself active through circular reaction with the external world and perhaps a few subsidiary coordinations. An object, the sensory input it aroused, and the motor outputs applied to it were all closely bound together; they were all the same structure and activity was concentrated in it. With higher coordinations and more complex structures, the activity of an element will tend to spread out through the network of elements. Control of activity and its confinement in any one structure will come to depend on well interconnected groups of elements. In a simple situation, one element could maintain its own reverberations through sensory feedback loops. In a more complex and diffuse system, only a well coordinated group can maintain its own reverberations.

The first order elements, as representations of objects, depended very much on direct sensory and motor activity. With second order elements, whole networks of the earlier representations become coordinated and differentiated to give multidimensional, multisensory, and multifunctional representations of real objects. Finally, with third order elements, it becomes possible to transfer activity from one part of a representation to another, even overriding contrary sensory inputs that would cause activity to transform somewhere else. These three levels or orders of representation are very similar to the enactive, ikonic, and symbolic representations discussed by Bruner (1966). With an eye to the future (at Stage Six, the child is only one or two years old), we might tentatively identify the process of differentiation and coordination as a kind of induction of structure into the nervous system from the external environment. A kind of deduction or working out of structure from the nervous system, and perhaps into the environment, is the invisible third order chaining from element to element and group to group. Induction is the developmental, and deduction is the functional aspect of elements of the model. With respect to the building block approach and the black box approach to the modeling of intelligence, the purely building block approach is weak at deduction or the transformation of the information (activities) contained in the building blocks. A purely black box approach is weak at induction or the creation of new structures to handle new information from the environment. Building block models seem unable to rise above the first level of representation representing pattern recognition, and the black box models seem unable to go below the level of the groups which represent internal images and symbolic processes. Building block models grow too complex to calculate all the details; systems models cannot pierce the top level of organization to the underlying structural details.

Conceptualization

Let's try to trace the development of concepts in the model. As a standard we will go back to Vygotsky's (1934) pioneering work in which he mapped out the stages in the conceptual development of children. Vygotsky used a collection of blocks of varying sizes, shapes, and colors. He would select a set of these blocks with certain common characteristics and label them on the bottom with some nonsense word. For example, one such set of blocks might consist of all blocks that were both tall and small in base area. The child who truly uses concepts should be able to make abstract combinations of such concepts as tall and small, and use this abstracted concept to sort the blocks into piles. For the experiment, Vygotsky would mix all the blocks together, select a single block, identify it to his subject by the name on its bottom, and ask his subject to pick out all the other blocks that might have the same name. (The subjects were not allowed to see the names on the bottom.) When the subject was done, the experimenter would pick up one of the blocks the subject had selected that wasn't labeled with the correct word, and reveal the error. The subject then tried again. More important than success was how the subject went about solving the problem, what cues he was able to use, and how he used the experimenter's revelations in the next attempt.

On the basis of his observations, Vygotsky divided conceptual development into three phases. Each phase in turn has several stages or types (the series of types is less strict in its sequence of development, the stage is more strict). In truth, a child's development does not really divide so sharply into phases and stages and types. Each phase grades long and slowly into the next. Nevertheless, Vygotsky's plan of conceptual development is outlined below with the approximate ages during which behavior typical of each phase predominates.

Phase I: Unorganized syncretic heaps. Dominates behavior till two or three years.
   Stage 1. Trial and error. Randomly the child puts another block with the demonstration block or accumulated heap.
   Stage 2. Spacial composition. The child forms a heap on the basis of proximity of blocks in the work area.
   Stage 3. Recombination. The child takes objects from previous heaps and forms new heaps; behavior is no longer a slave to one heap.

Phase II: Complexes. Uses any factual or sensory connection between a candidate block and the growing heap. Predominates from three to twelve years.

Type 1. Associative. A new block is added on the basis of similarity or contrast to some core block already in the heap.

Type 2. Collection. A set is formed in which the blocks contrast and complement each other (for example, a set of colors). The collection is determined by all blocks being used in one practical activity or sensory dimension.

Type 3. Chain. Blocks are selected for one property for awhile and then switched to some other property of some recently added block. There is no core block; adding a block may add all its properties to the heap.

Type 4. Diffuse. Blocks are added by similarity; for example, first black blocks and then blue, or first triangular shapes and then trapezoidal shapes are added to the heap. There is generalization of the selection property.

Type 5. Pseudo-concept. It appears a true concept is being used to select blocks, but, in fact, it is only a perceptual likeness. Nevertheless, the selecting property is held relatively constant and independent of the heap. This type is not a true concept because logical operations are not being made. For example, if a child has picked all red blocks and is shown that one of the red ones is in error, he does not abandon any other red blocks, he does not realize that red cannot then be the selecting property.

Phase III: Abstraction. Predominates behavior from twelve onwards.

Stage 1. Focusing of attention. Blocks are selected on a maximal likeness based on one or two properties.

Stage 2. Potential concepts. Selection is based on one attribute which is held constant. The attribute is not purely perceptual.

Stage 3. Concepts. The adolescent is able to abstract the correct properties and combine them; a new concept is synthesized anew for each task.

Long before reaching true conceptual behavior in Phase III, the child has structures that produce the behavior of complexes in Phase II. This is often enough to enable him to come to conclusions, to perform operations, and to make decisions that in fact match those reached by the adult. However, the true concept is not present until the child can perform logical operations with his concepts; for example, such a logical operation would be to form the combination of two different concepts and consistently select blocks that had only both conceptual properties. Thus, the structure representing a concept must be sufficiently crystallized and independent of sensory information to remain in control through several interactions with nonmatching blocks. Also, the concept structure must be sufficiently autonomous to be coordinated with other concept structures without being itself deformed or changed by its interaction with the other concept. Looking for tall blocks with small base areas must not alter the old concepts of tall or small too much. The new combined concept is a coordination and also a differentiation of each of the old ones which remain relatively unchanged. The new coordination and differentiation is a structure that is created by coordinating parts of the old structures; all the new elements stand between the two old structures as a coordinating structure and also reflect the structure of the old concepts as a differentiated structure. It is this new structure that includes the nonsense word given by the experimenter. Each old structure still may be used independently, much as they were used before, except now they have at their disposal a differentiated concept which, in some situations, may be aroused and found to match the environment, found to produce circular reaction. This kind of coordinating, differentiating new structure, may be useful in understanding how concepts can be formed into "hierarchies" of generalization. A more general concept is surrounded by a group of differentiated and coordinated structures; each structure is similar to the more general structure because each structure has some one-to-one correspondences between itself and the elements of the general structure. Each less general structure is different from the general structure by virtue of being also connected to a third structure. A more general structure might be formed by two processes: it could itself start as the coordination of two old structures which happen to match, that is, reverberate together easily. Later, through the process of differentiation (really the same as coordination, of course) partial copies of the general structure could be formed through coordination of the general structure to a new specific case, or to another general structure or concept. From Vygotsky's observations, it seems clear that the creation of concepts is not an immediate result of simply linking together the various substructures that define the concept; such simple linking merely results in the Phase II complexes. Only when the complexes become sufficiently large and self supporting can they maintain an independent existence; only when two of these large complexes can be quickly coordinated and differentiated into a new combined concept can true conceptual operations be made. Thus, the development of concepts out of complexes is a matter of degree, a matter of gradual increase in complex size until the criteria of autonomy and prompt differentiation can be met. Also, the increasing maturity of the attention span seems a prerequisite for the prompt coordination and differentiation of two structures; this increasing size of the attention span may be due to three processes: one, the attention may physically mature independent of the amount of learning that has occurred; two, the increasing number of elements may simply increase the effective attention span by affecting the activity-reverberation ratio; and, three, the early cell assemblies may be very large, and, by progressive differentiation, they become smaller as to the number of cells actually involved—if attention span is physiologically a constant number of cells involved in reverberation, then more cell assemblies may fit into the same sized attention span as the average size of the cell assembly decreases. In short, the development of concepts is very similar to the development of short term memory, only now the structures involved are much larger and more numerous. Let's trace Vygotsky's sequence of conceptual development to see this process. (Because of the strong sensorimotor nature of Vygotsky's block sorting task, the development of six short term memory structures as hypothesized at the end of Chapter Two is not involved, only the increasing autonomy of a few; in the earlier hypothesis, the task being modeled was more in the nature of a mental solution to some proposed problem.)

In Phase I there is not much more than a sensorimotor structure for manipulating the blocks and arranging them in piles. This structure acts by itself and is insensitive to the differences in the blocks; it is undifferentiated and treats all blocks as one thing. The manipulating structure cannot (because of attention span?) function in coordination with some other sensory structure for recognizing some property of the blocks. The first use of spacial composition or previous heaps represents a first differentiation of the structure to distinguish between different parts of the working space and different piles of blocks. The earliest short term memories would likely be closely related to such spacial memories involving orientations in different spacial directions. For the most part, this stage represents the simple exercise of the manipulating structure. That the child can maintain interest in the activity long enough to collect a heap, may at first depend on simple circular reaction with the environment. Towards the end of this stage, some form of short term memory (still closely related to the dominate motor activity) may help maintain and direct interest.

In Phase II, the manipulating structures become sensitive to differences in the blocks; not only does the manipulating structure of hand-eye coordination function, but, also, additional structures are influencing the manipulating structure's sensitivity to the blocks. For example, if the child has just looked at his sample block and notices it is red (certain perceptual elements are set to reverberating), then when he looks back at the mixed blocks, the red ones will attract his attention—they will increase activity in already reverberating structures and produce a defense response; activities go up, concentration is narrowed down, and the reaching structure is made active enough to initiate a movement in the direction the child is already looking: the red block is seized. In Phase II, blocks are placed together because they arouse similar structures, or because they happen to fit the function of some particular structure that is currently in command (reverberating). However, the child is unable to hold this structure very long; it drifts, changes, and is replaced by others suggested by the environment or by internal coordinations (as in Type 2 collections and, perhaps, Type 4 diffusion). The structures are not yet grouped enough, self-facilitating enough to maintain themselves in control for very long. Towards the end of Phase II, with the Type 5 pseudo-concepts, the structures can maintain themselves in control through extended periods of time and contact with contrary sensory stimulations, but they cannot be logically (i.e., independently of sensorimotor activities) coordinated and recombined into new structures.

In Phase III, the child is finally able to focus or maintain his attention on a particular structure for an extended period of time. The possibility of consistently using a combination of two different structures throughout the trial first emerges. Degrees of match are now recognized as the structures used for selection criteria become more complex and differentiated. Information returned by the experimenter can be used formally (that is, without any reference to relevant sensorimotor structures of perception and procedure; a few verbalizations can formally, through internal connections, select new visual criteria). Finally, the adolescent can quickly form new combinations of concepts out of the old (remember the mental recombinations of the one year old child). The attainment of true concepts implies the groups have been sufficiently well formed and interrelated among themselves to allow their use as a consistent (repeatable from memory without sensory aids) basis of operations. New groups can be quickly formed from old ones by coordinations and differentiations among the old ones. Logical transformations (that is, transformations directed by internal structure) from group to group are possible and sensitive to which elements are facilitated along the way (for example, facilitated by a few words from the experimenter). All this kind of "logical" transformation occurred with the complexes (especially with sensory aid, or distraction); the concept is different, being more stable and more dependent on internal structure. Where changes in complex selection criteria depended on sensory activity; changes in conceptual selection criteria can depend more on reverberations in other structures, short term memories, as in the case of creation of new differentiated concepts, or formal mediating structures, as in the case of the use of the experimenter's feedback.

To summarize the development of concepts, an event in the environment is represented by an element, a coordination of all the channels through which activity is flowing at the time of the event. This is the lowest level of organization. Next, these elements are linked together to form complexes, higher order structures involving a number of elements and paths for activity to flow from element to element. The various events brought together in a complex may represent the internal image of an object, a template for a motor skill, or any system of events that the external environment may present to the child. Complex data structures lead to the formation of complex heaps in Phase II of the block task. Finally, these complex structures increase in size and organization until their self-integrity and self-sufficiency is enough to allow them to interact with other structures (internal, or in the environment) in a consistent, predictable, and independent manner. Whole structures can be coordinated quickly and easily to form new, derived structures. And as these internal structures develop, the kind of circular reaction they can support moves from the very simple reflexive circular reaction to a very complex circular reaction, as involved in the scientific method; collect inputs or data, process to devise a theory (accommodate the data structures to fit the data), play with the theory to discover some predictions (allow reverberations to move about the new structures until some unexpected result is found), carry out an experiment (perform motor actions), and repeat the process. Even at Stage Five, this is essentially what the infant was doing in active experimentation. At an advanced level of conceptual inventions the same process takes place, only then the complex circular reaction is completely internalized; one system of structures acts as the internal representation of the environment, and the other system of structures acts as the developing hypothesis.

Finally, if we step back far enough and change our scale of observation, we might consider each strongly interconnected group of elements as a single complex element. Each concept then is represented by a single element, and the Fig. 18's sort of structure might result. Each concept is surrounded by a set of

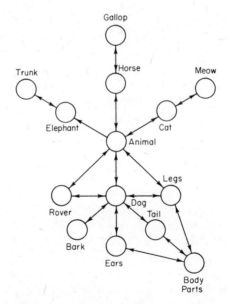

Fig. 18. The hierarchy of concepts is more illusion than reality. (The concept "ears" shown here is really a differentiated concept "dog ears.")

differentiated concepts, defining concepts, or otherwise related concepts. There are hierarchies of generalization such as the sequence "animal," "dog," "Rover;" there is a hierarchy of specification such as the group "legs," "tail," "bark" that surrounds "dog." The concept "dog" is differentiated from the concept "animal" by virtue of its connections with other concepts. The structure in Fig. 18 is misleading; "tail" might also be directly connected to the central concept "animal." In reality, the structure of Fig. 18 would be much more interconnected than shown; the hierarchical structure is only in relation to yet other concepts, only one of which is shown in Fig. 18, the concept "parts." Activity of the concept "dog" and the concept "parts" results in activity of the hierarchically related parts of the dog. Thus, the real data structure has no hierarchy, the mind moves from "dog" to "Rover" by the same process it moves from "dog" to "animal" or to "bark." It is only a particular situation (usually an experimental situation) that provides the extra cues that cause a hierarchy to emerge for the moment: two structures in first level memory cause several structures to rise to second level memory. Even the division into concepts may be more illusion than reality. An individual element may participate in several different groups of interlinked elements; concepts intersect rather than interlink. A particular concept may just be another way of cutting the pie; given a few cues in first level memory, enough additional elements are retrieved for a short term memory to be established. Given some other cues, some of the same elements may be retrieved as before, in addition to a few different ones, and these, together, set up a short term memory. Short term memory is the primordial concept: a memory structure that can be independent of sensory input and can independently impose itself on the environment through motor outputs, a memory structure that can interact with other memory structures just as the environment once interacted with these other memory structures. Vygotsky withholds the title "concept" until the short term memory structure is so complex that it becomes stable and relatively immune to further development; perhaps it becomes so large and complex that only small parts of it are needed at a time to establish short term memory and any coordinations formed only to these parts leaves the rest unchanged. Still, the new coordination has implicitly, through internal chaining, the whole of the conceptual structure connected to it. Finally, if the data structure is so interconnected, how is the boundary of a concept to be defined? Is "dog" a part of the concept "animal?" Does it only partially intersect? Are they only linked? If we don't know its internal workings, the concept as a unitary whole is a black box construct we infer from behavioral data. In a building block model, the movement from one cell assembly to the next, to the next, to the next, is much more graded; if we don't know when we cross the boundary between concepts, then it doesn't really exist.

Language

If we are able to use the cell assembly model for language at all, it will have to be as a theory of language performance, of verbal language as it is actually used. Such formal theories as Chomsky's (1965) phrase structure and transformational grammars are theories of idealized and abstract competence, black box theories imposed from without. In the cell assembly model, development must result in structures that can produce the behavior which the black box theories describe in part. Most formal studies of language divide language into two systems: the sequential structure or syntax of language, and the meaning or semantics of language. In addition, there are sometimes practical or pragmatic considerations that set limits on the length and complexity of language.

The fact that language can carry meaning between two users of the language is due to the internal structures of the users, and not due to the linguistic utterances or texts themselves. If linguistic meaning exists at all, or is of any significance or consequence in the world, then it exists and is of consequence in the human mind. Words and sentences have meaning, as does the cell assembly itself, only in terms of the mental structures that produce and recognize them, that "facilitate" and are "facilitated" by them. If we insist on meaning having a physical representation and not being merely a formal abstraction (the cell assembly model insists on physical representation for mind, it should insist on as much for meaning), then the meaning of a word is the structure that produces or recognizes the word, and, more generally, all the structures coordinated to that structure.

The internal representation, the meaning of a word, is built up by the experiences which are presumably common to all humans; hence, there is some degree of communication between individuals. Verbalizing a word that is part of a certain structure is a convenient way of arousing some roughly similar structure in another person. The semantics of language and thought are one and the same in the cell assembly model. The meaning of a particular structure is the other structures which it can arouse and which arouse it; meaning is the context, setting, or supporting superstructure of the particular structure. At first, for a very young child, the word is treated as if it were actually an attribute, just as the visual image is an attribute, of the object named; mountains are called mountains because that's what they are. (See for example, Observation 123 of Piaget's *Play, Dreams, and Imitation,* 1962). Later, as the word structure is coordinated to yet other words and other semantic structures, and as the child uses these coordinations, the word gains a certain independent existence (just as the internal representations of objects become objectified and independent of any one sensorimotor activity) and becomes a symbol—a handle for the semantic group of structures of which the word is a part, and a handle through which the social experience of language can manipulate and change that semantic group.

The word structure is the connection between two different systems; on the one hand, the system of representations of the environment, and, on the other hand, the system of coordinations that string words together in motor production or interpret them in a stream of auditory stimulation. The first system is semantics and thought, the second system is syntax and language. Sometimes thought precedes and directs language, and sometimes language precedes and directs thought, both developmentally and functionally. At times the two systems (really one) function and develop together. Language as it is actually produced is directed by thought, but language as a social experience molds thought into communicable structures standard for a particular society. Only so far as we have already discussed conceptualization and the general thought processes in terms of the model, let us assume we have already covered the semantics of language performance.

The most striking aspect of language (aside from its ability to carry meaning) is its strictly sequential order. This order is imposed on it by the inability of the vocal tract to take on more than one shape at a time. (This one at a time order may be violated by the use of intonation, stress, or pitch parallel with articulation; but for now let's ignore this.) The problem for the child is to learn to order his normal thought processes, which are richly multiple and parallel, into this sequential mode. The earliest example of this is, perhaps, the formation of single words when auditory feedback of each sound being produced helps produce the next sound in sequence. Higher order coordinations sequence the lower order procedures and perceptions which produce and recognize the elementary units of speech. These higher order structures represent the word as something distinct from the sounds out of which it is made; these higher order structures are in turn coordinated to other high order structures to give a word its semantic connection to other sensorimotor structures and its syntactic connection to other word and speech structures. (Herein lies the duality of patterning, a linguistic universal suggested by Hockett.)

Sequential ordering is a universal; it applies to all human languages. However, each language has its own set of sequential conventions that assign special meanings to some sequences, forbid others, and make yet others obligatory or preferred. One part of linguistics attempts to discover all these conventions and summarize them in a set of rules or a phrase structure grammar for the language. The linguistic universal of sequential ordering stipulates only that we can say "A" and then "B," or "B" and then "A," but never can we say both "A" and "B" at exactly the same time. On the other hand, the conventions of a particular language may stipulate that we can say "A B," but not "B A," or it may stipulate that "A B" has some particular meaning (elements it can arouse) that "B A" hasn't. For the discussion here, let's call a set of sounds or words whose order is determined by the sequence conventions of a language, a phrase.

Beyond the sequence conventions of a language, phrases, words, or sounds may be arranged in any order—that much is left to the individual taste of the speaker. In practice, the ordering of phrases is used to give emphasis (the first part of an utterance), style (individual idiosyncracies), ease of production and comprehension (by placing together related phrases). Beyond emphasis, style, and clarity, any possible ordering should allow the same meaning or interpretation. In linguistics this has been expressed by saying there are transformations between utterances that have no semantic difference. There are also transformations which may change the meaning of a sentence by changing some of its words, phrases, or sounds. But, for us, changes in meaning are semantic problems and a semantically different utterance presumably is generated by a semantically different starting point (set of reverberating structures). The transformations of the cell assembly model transform activity from one set of elements to another, perhaps along a rather complicated pathway of links and elements, and perhaps producing motor outputs and utterances along the way. The transformation of formal grammars are not in the brain; they are the description of the existence of two or more utterances or classes of utterances with a given semantic difference (or perhaps none). A single transformation of formal grammar tries to describe the difference between two different transformations of the model, transformations which start with the same set of reverberating elements (or perhaps slightly different sets).

An interpretation of syntax must address itself to the following problem: a speaker has a certain set of reverberating structures (or meaning) in mind which is to be verbalized. Coordinated with these structures will be certain other structures for producing words and sequences of sounds. In a language with no sequence conventions these words would be produced one at a time in a seemingly random order that was, in fact, determined by the idiosyncrasies of the individual speaker. However, all languages do in fact have some sequence restrictions, and if the speaker was careful and had learned those restrictions (that is, if he had developed his mental structures only as his linguistic experiences allowed) then his utterance would conform to these restrictions with the rest of the word order determined by his individual style, emphasis, and fancy (and confusions). Most speakers are not too careful and errors, restarts, and parenthetical digressions are common. From the other side, a listener presumably has the standard words of the language already coordinated with other structures in his mind, and even a randomly arranged utterance of these words should arouse some of these structures. (Certainly a theory of performance must account for the comprehension of ungrammatical utterances. One of the difficulties for formal grammars is that they must try to specify all the permutations that the sequence conventions don't prohibit, or that the mind can accept.) However, the better the arrangement of words in an utterance fits a listener's expectations, the better he will understand and the more congruent his final set of aroused structures will be with those of the speaker (assuming that their common linguistic experience has, in fact, molded their internal structures similarly). The listener's expectations of sequence are defined by his own internalization of the sequence conventions of his language; given the utterance he is listening to, if his internal coordinations pass activity smoothly on from element to element, then all is well. But, if not, he may be surprised; his attention span may be increased and new coordinations formed. If the discrepancy is too great, the elements brought to first level memory may have few connections with the elements already there, or may replace too many of the old elements; meaning is lost and confusion results. If the discrepancy is slight, then only a few elements strange to the contents of first level memory are aroused and coordinated; a neat turn of phrase is picked up.

In studies of children's first grammars (*The Acquisition of Language,* 1964, edited by Bellugi and Brown), the first chance that sequence restrictions have to show themselves occurs when the child begins to string two words together. The first sequence restrictions almost invariably show up as a certain word used by the child in a fixed position of several different utterances. Such a word is first used by the child in a fairly consistent manner, either at the beginning or at the end of a two word utterance. Usually, when a study is first made of a child's grammar, he already has a small set of these "pivot" words and a rather larger set of "open" words which seem to be used without preference at either the beginning or the end of an utterance, depending on the positional property of the pivot word with which it is used. When the pivot comes at the beginning of the utterance, it might be called a pre-positional (a term invented for our discussion here, and not necessarily related to the class of words called prepositions). An example of pre-positional would be the word "see" in such utterances as "See Mommy," "See glasses," "See cat," where the second word is chosen from the set of open words in the child's vocabulary. When the pivot word comes consistently at the end of an utterance, it might be called a postpositional; an example would be "———off," where the blank is filled from the set of open words to give such utterances as "Sweater off," "Hat off," "Chair off." Of course the two word utterances produced by a child's first pre- and postpositional structures may not be grammatically correct by adult standards, and often the two word utterances produced will have no model in the adult language of which they might be an imitation. But, once a positional structure is established, through generalization and chaining, it may be used with many different words in the variable position, and without regard for precedence in adult examples.

In the cell assembly model of elements and links, a pre-positional word would be one that was most aroused at the beginning of an utterance. It could be facilitated by the actual intake of breath in preparation for an utterance. Or it could simply be a word that was very easily aroused by internal structures not related to speech. For instance, the word "see" might be aroused by the activity of the eye coordinations, even without earlier speech activity. Thus, the increased activity of visual tracking and, perhaps, hand-eye coordinations for pointing that result from seeing an interesting sight could start the speech production of the word "see." Then, having started speech activities, other words could be added on—especially words coordinated to recognitory structures for the visual image. Finally, there may be a functional and structural interaction that causes a word to be used as a pre-positional; if several structures for different words are brought to first level memory and maintained there as short term memory, then, as the defense response begins to narrow down the attention span and increase activities, some word structures may be better self-facilitating than others and they would be the first to build up enough activity to initiate motor production. Then, as attention span narrows further, large structures might fail and leave first level memory to smaller structures that finally take control of motor production. In this respect, it is interesting to note that two word productions do not begin until the child has entered the sixth stage of sensorimotor development and has the capacity to handle two short term memories simultaneously. Of course, the postpositionals would be structures with the obvious inverse characteristics of the pre-positionals, and the open words would be a mixture of the pre-positional and postpositional. To summarize, the positional nature of a word in speech production may be a result of its connections to other structures which then influence its position in an utterance, and also may be a result of the size and compactness of the structure that produces the word.

The above hypothesis about the nature of word position would suggest that the child does not have a single structure for all his pre-positionals and another one for all his postpositionals. Rather, the structure for each word itself has positional properties inherent in the links from other structures and in its own structure. The child's internal representation for a word might become pre-positional by hearing it often at the beginning of adult speech or as the first recognizable thing in an adult utterance. Or, having a word closely related to some activity independent of speech could establish that word as a pre-positional; it becomes the entry to speech activity from the other activity (or perception) to which it is closely related. Another way a word could become pre-positional would be the use of that word as the initial segment of two different "words" or sequences of sounds that the child has picked up independently and used as separate one "word" utterances. Discovering that each of the utterances has an identical initial segment, the two initial segments may become coordinated and produce an initial word structure that is relatively large and therefore has pre-positional properties. Such a discovery may occur when the child hears the initial segment in adult speech; both structures are brought to first level memory together and coordinated. Or the child may begin to produce one of the "words," but through sensory feedback arouses the structures of the other "word." The initial segment of the two old "words" is differentiated and coordinated out of the old structures and assumes an independent existence—it becomes a word, and a word with the pre-positional properties inherent in being the initial segment of the two old words and in being relatively complex and likely to arouse motor production with less defense response. In a similar manner, postpositional words could be established by hearing them as the last recognizable part of an adult utterance or discovering them as the common end of two different phrases. In either case the word would likely be coordinated to other word structures just heard and still reverberating, and would depend somewhat on those words for facilitation. As the child's speech matures, the facilitations of pre- and postpositionals may come increasingly from intonations and stress which are a natural part of beginning and ending an utterance and which are therefore coordinated to the various word structures; respiratory reflexes must also be involved in word productions if breathing is to be controlled while a word is produced. Stress, intonations, and a residual pause thus may allow pre- and postpositionals deep with an adult's long utterance. The close relation between respiratory variation and changes in the attention span have been discussed before. We might envision attention span going up as a set of words to be uttered are collected, and then going down as they are run off in the sequence dictated by their interconnections and internal structure. Then when the words have been produced and crowded out of first level memory by the falling attention span, the point would be reached where the attention span would begin going up again because of the loss of reverberating elements. New structures would crowd onto first level memory, there would be a respiratory pause, and a new sweep through attention span would begin starting with the structure that most facilitates the motor elements used in word production. The new elements brought to first level memory would be brought up from second level memory by the elements remaining in first level memory when the defense response failed and was replaced by an orienting response. Word structures were crowded off the attention span and verbalized. Finally, the only ones left could produce no more words—they were not word structures—and they facilitated relatively many elements in second level memory, thus causing an orienting response when attention span was narrowed down to them.

Once a child has positionals, we can see how more complex structures may evolve. A pre-positional only starts speech, it does not determine necessarily the next word. In fact, the structure of a pre-positional does not even determine that only one word may follow. At first the child's shortness of breath and attention span may limit the length of his utterances, but, as breath control develops, his utterances may lengthen to three and more words. Thus, the open spaces in the positional phrases may be filled by yet other phrases, and not just words. A fairly complicated phrase structure grammar might develop using only the two positional structures.

A rather difficult problem in formal grammars (and one that is solved in part by transformational type grammars) is the agreement of different parts of a sentence in terms of number, tense, gender, or other basically semantic distinctions. These are not sequence restrictions and they cannot be accounted for simply by the phrasing produced by pre-positional and postpositional structures. Still they fit in with the general model developed here. An utterance is generated by the activity of a certain image, idea, or set of structures and elements. As an utterance is generated, it is interacting with the nonspeech structures which are also reverberating, perhaps throughout the course of the utterances. These nonspeech structures direct the course of the utterance, and, as a result, the utterance becomes something of a description of them, a linguistic impression of them. It is a fixed set of cognitive structures, reverberating throughout the entire utterance, that guides the selection of words and sounds in a consistent manner so that different parts of the utterance (or even a long series of utterances) agree in number, person, tense, and the like. As an example, consider the pronoun.

Quite early the child makes use of pronouns in his simple utterances. These pronouns are often pivots of a positional structure. He often places them in correct sequential order with respect to other words, perhaps because of their frequent use there in adult speech. There are also other words whose positional structure allows them to be used in the same places as the pronouns. Often a conflict emerges and an utterance such as "Daddy he gone" is produced. Eventually, the child will be able to select definitely one word or the other on the basis of which is more active or better cued, but two important results follow from this early positional conflict. First, the child develops some coordinations between the pronouns and the nouns that may occur in their place. Thus, the pronouns may be likely to coordinate to most nouns by virtue of the fact that the pronouns and the nouns may at times be generated (made to reverberate) together, at least subvocally, as in the observed example "Daddy he gone." The resultant simultaneity of "Daddy" and "he" may establish a coordination between them, and since the pronoun "he" may be generated with less dependence on its meaning than most nouns, it may turn up quite often and become coordinated to many nouns. The pronoun may become the center of a highly differentiated and coordinated group of structures representing all the nouns. The second result of positional conflict follows from this complex structure for the nouns; the pronoun is indeed a proto-noun; the child has only to learn the sequence restrictions for the pronoun and then all the nouns, once coordinated with the pronoun, will tend to have the same restrictions although not explicitly learned. Finally, as a matter of developmental history, it is probably wrong to consider the pronoun as a substitute for a noun in a sentence. Rather, it is the pronoun which "naturally" occurs, and only at important semantic points, with extra cues to help, is the activity of the noun structure strong enough to replace the pronoun.

Weir (1962) has made a study of her own two-and-one-half-year-old child's presleep monologues. The time just before a child falls asleep, in a darkened room, and with a minimum of sensory distraction, would seem ideal for studying the inner structure of the child's speech patterns. In normal, daily life, the child's sensory perceptions, and especially what he hears others saying, could have a very strong influence on his own verbalizations, but in the presleep monologue such external influences are at a minimum. That the presleep monologues occur should not be surprising; the infant perhaps sucked his thumb and this constant mild motor activity depressed attention span and helped induce sleep. For the slightly older child, talking to himself might have the same cause and effect.

In Weir's study, there are three aspects of the child's speech which seem to be related to attention span. These were termed build up, break down, and completion. Examples of build up would be "Daddy. Daddy bucket please." Or in another case, "Donkey. Fix the donkey." Examples of break down would be be "Anthony jump out again. Anthony jump." or "Another big bottle. Big bottle." Finally, examples of completion are "And put it. Up there." "Anthony take the. Take the book."

Build up seems to consist of the selection of a topic, and then an elaboration on that topic. In the cell assembly model, the topic selected, as evidenced by its verbal productions, is the most active structure currently in the child's mind. As the reverberations in the structure increase to the point that they produce verbalizations, they also increase the amount of activity going to structures in second level memory. In addition, the sensory feedback of auditory stimulations may further facilitate second level structures. In any event, an orienting response is produced and more structures are brought onto first level memory where they are, so to speak, sorted out according to their relative activities and produce a new sequence of words. When more mature, the child may use this same process to string out longer sentences composed of clauses or phrases, each introduced by an initial topical utterance, followed by a pause, and, finally, by an expanded utterance.

Where build up might be viewed as a gradual increase or spread of the number of reverberating structures, break down might be the opposite: a dying away of some of the less active structures, leaving only the most strongly facilitated topical structures in first level memory for a second utterance. In build up, the central structure of a group of structures (that is, a structure coordinated to each of a group of structures) is aroused and verbalized, followed by the spread of reverberations to some of the other structures in the group. In break down, the process of verbalization pushes some of the reverberating structures out of first level memory. In the second utterance, only those structures that best supported each other are able to remain in first level memory. In the example given above, the words "Anthony jump" are clearly more likely to have meaning to the child, to be of greater interest and importance to him, and to be coordinated together anyway, than the words "out again."

Between build up and break down, there is repetition where the child repeats the same utterance over and over. In Weir's study, this repetition occurs quite frequently and in especially prolonged cases, it perhaps degenerates into a simple circular reaction. Also, there are many examples where break down is followed again by build up; the remaining structures that produce the second utterance might then have coordinations with the other structures that can therefore be retrieved for the third utterance.

Finally, in completion we see where the child is able to bridge the breathtaking gap and, in two utterances, generate a more complex sentence. The instability of the structures is not so great that they cannot maintain control of first level memory through two utterances. Completion is really a chaining together of two utterances, perhaps by some words common to both or by some common semantic connection. Build up and break down also represent a sort of chaining or transformation of reverberation from structure to structure, but completion represents something a bit more advanced. The two utterances of a completion form a whole (by adult standards anyway) that is greater than either of its parts.

The underlying structures that permit chaining to occur can be of several types. The following are some examples of the types of chains identified by Weir:

Sound:	"Babette. Back here. Wet."
Antonyms:	"Up there. Over here."
Associations:	"Like the garbage man. A big truck."
Question-answer:	"What color TV? Red and."
Negation:	"Not yellow. Red."
Substitution:	"What color. What color blanket. What color map."
	"Stop it. Stop the ball. Stop it."
Transformation:	"Fix the music. Music is fixed."
Enumeration:	"And monkey and horsie. And vacuum cleaner."

In each of the examples above we can readily guess what the common structure between utterances might be. In the sound chain it is the structure for recognizing and producing the sounds "ba" and "et." In the association chain it is whatever structure represents the memory of the garbage man with his big truck. In the question and answer chain, the common structure between the two utterances is the memory of the TV and its coordination to color recognition structures. In the antonym chain, it is some group or dimension along which the words vary—words with similar positional structure that are perhaps coordinated together as the nouns and pronouns are coordinated together. In the negation chain, structures for recognizing colors are common to both utterances. In the substitution chains, the common structure is a single positional word or phrase. In the transformation chain we can see how the two words "music" and "fix" connect the two utterances; the word "music" is repeated immediately, and whatever postpositional words come to mind are added on.

In summary, we have been able to loosely interpret in the cell assembly model the sequential restrictions of language as a sort of phrase structure grammar built up from two kinds of positional structures. A way for interpreting the division of words of a language into syntactic classes such as noun and verb has been sketched for the case of the pronoun and the class of nouns. The semantic organization of language has been postulated to be inherent in the functional rules of the model and the data structure built up from experience. Instead of transformations from one syntactic form to another (as in formal grammars), in this model the transformations are of activity from some initial structure through a sequence of structures that produce the utterance. The child moves from utterance to utterance, indeed from thought to thought, because some of the reverberating structures are dropped and others picked up, a process controlled jointly by the nature of the structures themselves through their effect on the reverberation ratio and by the cognitive reflexes which maintain the reverberation ratio within certain bounds. Utterances are made self consistent and given coherence by a few mental structures that remain active throughout the generation of an utterance or a sequence of utterances. Finally, language has the power of communication because of the similarity of the language (and other perceptual and procedural) structures for all speakers of the language, a similarity induced by common social experience.

Computer Implementation

So far, the terms "cell assembly" and "element" have been nearly synonymous. This is an unnecessary confusion perhaps, but there have been several reasons for it. The first has been something of a confusion in my own mind; in the beginning I felt a need to avoid confusion by having two separate terms, one for the presumed physical reality, and one for the developing formalism. However, I find now that the two concepts have been interacting and gradually merging into one (through the process of accommodation, or coordination and differentiation, no doubt). Unfortunately, my initial separation and then confusion of these two terms (together with several other systems of what turned out to be synonymous concepts) may prove to be something of a stumbling block to the unwary reader. However, to go back now, and rationally, consistently distinguish between the two terms would be too laborious, so I have decided to let them stand. Besides, if anything is clear by now, it is that learning proceeds precisely by such a process of confusion and elaboration of two different systems. If the reader has any understanding now of what has been said, then it is not the mere result of linguistic consistency; hopefully an understanding of the crossed terms "cell assembly" and "element" will extend well beyond the mere concrete reality of the one and the formal abstraction of the other. Just as the child's coordination of hand and eye gave an entirely new meaning to the visual image of his hand (and other peoples' hands), so the coordination of Hebb's (1949), Piaget's (1936), and Sokolov's (1963) studies (to name only the three most important) will hopefully provide new meaning and insight into the one reality that lies behind them all. Some confusion of terms is perhaps necessary to surprise and force the reader to make accommodations and create anew an understanding; it was for me. (I had intended to go back and completely rationalize the terminology of this book; now I am tempted to go back and add useful confusions.) In any event, there is now some point in this section to have two different terms: "cell assembly" and "element." Having confounded them, we can now distinguish them. Where a cell assembly is supposed to be a complex physical reality, a system of neurons in the brain, the element is a simple abstracted unit of code and processor (information and information processor together at once) that might be implemented or simulated on a computer without regard for the complexities of neurophysiology.

In a computer implementation of the model, there might be a useful division into five subsystems as shown in Fig. 19: an input interface to play the role of sensory receptors in translating environmental information into activities of input elements, an output interface to play the role of muscles which translate internal activities into environmental forms of information (force and movement), the data structure for containing a description of all the elements of

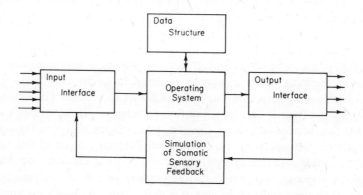

Fig. 19. Block diagram of information flow for a computer simulation.

the model together with their interconnections, the operating system for regulating the flow of activity or information through the data structure, and, finally, a computer simulation of the feedback from output to input which is normally carried out by the body.

Each element of the data structure would be assigned an address in the computer's memory and would consist of nothing more than a list of the addresses of all the other elements which it facilitates, to which its links point. Whenever a new element was to be created, an unused portion of the computer memory would be set up to represent the new element; old elements with links to this new element would have the address of this portion of memory added to their list of addresses, the old elements to which the new element has links would have their addresses stored in this portion of memory. An address is the computer's equivalent of link.

Those elements that happened to be input elements would be kept in a table in the input interface. The input interface would receive symbolic inputs from whatever input devices were being used in the simulation (perhaps, simply, a typewriter giving strings of typed characters representing stimulation of various simulated sensory receptors). Upon receiving a symbolic input character, the input interface would look this character up in a table and find the address of the sensory input element that is supposed to be aroused by this input. The address of this element would be passed to the operating system along with an activity. (Different symbolic input characters might arouse different input elements to varying degrees of activity.)

The operating system would maintain a constantly changing list of the addresses of the elements with high enough activity to be reverberating. In theory, each element is a tiny processor which collects activity and tries to pass activity down its links. However, the only elements and links that matter are those that actually reach reverberation. Rather than having the computer sweep through the data structure and update the activity of each element, it would be less work to have it consider only those that are reverberating. These elements may be selected from among those passed to the operating system by the input interface; they may also be memory elements found active enough by the operating system to be reverberating. Now, only those elements actually on the list of reverberating elements need be retrieved from memory. The operating system will look up these elements and their list of addresses of linked elements. Having done that, it is then in a position to calculate the activities of all the elements that receive facilitation from the reverberating elements. Once that is accomplished, the operating system can calculate how much of the total of activity is in elements already in its list of reverberating elements. An orienting or defense response may be necessary; the size of the list of reverberating elements is changed and the amount of activity passed by a link is changed (to be used in the next cycle of calculation of activities). Finally, a new set of elements for the reverberating list is selected from those elements just calculated to have the highest activities (including the list of active input elements just passed to the operating system by the input interface). Newly reverberating elements are looked up in memory, and all activities calculated again. The process repeats itself endlessly.

With each new list of reverberating first level memory, the computer will check to see if the conditions for creating new elements are met, and, if so, the appropriate new elements will be created and placed into the data structure. Also, the computer will check the active elements for output elements and, if any are found, their addresses will be passed on to the output interface. In the output interface there will be a table of all the output elements' addresses and the corresponding output that is to be given for different levels of activity in that element. Performing the translation from input activities to output responses, the output interface will produce some symbolic output on an output device of the computer (again, perhaps a typewriter). The environment (someone sitting at the typewriter) may respond by giving a new set of inputs. Finally, there may be some very automatic feedback from output to input (such as auditory feedback from vocal responses or kinesthetic feedback from motor responses) which can be simulated by the computer, again by looking up in a table the feedback corresponding to each output produced. Such simulated feedback simply make the job of the person sitting at the typewriter (or whatever environment is being used in the simulation) much easier.

Of course, the computer cannot perform the operations for all five subsystems at once. It will have to divide its time between them, first carrying out the processes of one system, and then the next, and the next, in a cyclic fashion. A flowchart for the simulation is shown in Fig. 20. The structure of the elements, lists, and tables used in a simulation are suggested in Fig. 21.

There are several reasons for believing that today's computer could handle this simulation of the enormous capacity of the brain for processing and storage. First of all, it is not necessary that all the input and output channels of the human being be simulated—intelligence develops in the deaf and blind. By cutting the initial input and output elements to a minimum necessary for communication and awareness of some environment of discourse, the magnitude of a simulation even of language development may come with the range of present day capacities. Second, nowhere does intelligence seem to depend on the exact nature of inputs and outputs, only so long as they interact with the environment. It is intelligence which discovers the exact nature of the inputs and outputs and their interrelations through the environment, whatever they are. We are free to choose our simulation's input and output within the limits set by DS1 through DS7. Instead of tens of thousands of auditory inputs and vocal tract motor effectors, we might as well choose to have a single input and output for each letter in the alphabet, or perhaps for each word; thus, a great deal of early

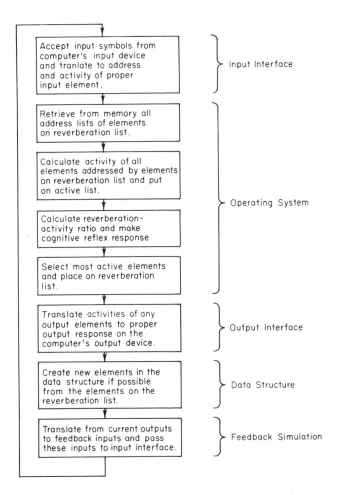

Fig. 20. A macro flow chart for a computer simulation.

development might be bypassed so that clearly linguistic behavior might be reached earlier. The sensorimotor basis may vary, but intelligence itself remains constant and defined by its functional, structural, and developmental characteristics. Finally, by concentrating on a limited environment, intelligent behavior may develop faster with less distraction and complication, and with less total growth needed before higher order structures emerge.

In fact, the use of the computer may be twofold; first is to abstract and recreate intelligent behavior (as assumed in the preceding paragraph); second may be to test the predictions of various hypotheses about the nature of learning, mental retardation, and malfunction. Any theory that could be

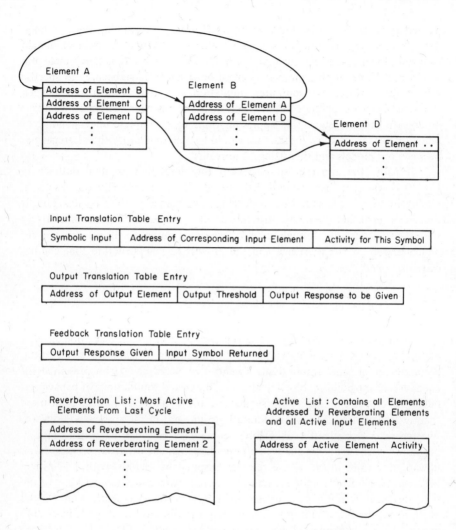

Fig. 21. Data used in a computer simulation.

incorporated into the formalization might be tested on the computer. For example, different training procedures could be tried on identical initial models. Such parameters as the size of the attention span, the reverberation ratios for producing defense and orienting responses, the relative activities of motor, sensory, and memory elements, and the rate of maturation could be varied, and the effect on development and function could be observed. While not a proof of any sort, a congruence between observed human behavior and simulated computer behavior for changes in such parameters would be most suggestive. Of particular value would be the possibility of directly examining the simulated data structure that produces a simulated behavior congruent to observed human behavior. Finally, it is certain that the model presented here is incomplete and inaccurate. None of the parameters mentioned above have been given specific values. By a process of computer simulation and then comparison between simulated behavior of the computer and observed behavior of humans we might be able to produce successive approximations to a complete understanding of human behavior; at the very least we would be able to identify the discrepancies between our models and theorizings, and reality.

Finally, the apparent simplicity of the simulation program outlined in Fig. 20 is genuine; there is very little to it. All the complexity out of which intelligent behavior is supposed to develop is contained in the data structure. It is Piaget's claim that the innate structure and function of intelligence is relatively simple and constant throughout life; we must hope so if we are ever to understand it. It is experience and the growth of new structure that complicates us.

Summary: No Conclusions, and Confession

Thirty-six years ago Piaget (1936) presented his brilliant black box analysis of the beginnings of intelligence in children: a model of schemata, assimilation, accommodation, and equilibrium. Twenty-two years ago Hebb presented his equally brilliant building block analysis of the neural foundations of behavior: a model of cell assemblies, phase sequences, and cycles. Since then, both these theories have suffered from the limitations inherent in the approach they used. The growing complexity of Hebb's complexes of building blocks rapidly becomes impenetrable to our feeble understanding; cut off from progress in an upward direction, much of the research inspired by Hebb's work, has instead been directed towards understanding the detailed structure and workings of the individual cell assembly as a neurological or psychological abstraction. On the other hand, the impossibility of penetrating the top level of Piaget's black box analysis to the detailed workings underneath has resulted in most of the research inspired by Piaget's work being directed towards even higher and higher systems of behavior: concrete and formal operations, logic systems, stages, and conservation. In addition, it seems as though Hebb's work has been partly discredited by the research (after the writing of *The Organization of Behavior*) on pain and pleasure centers in the brain—obvious (too obvious) neural bases for motivation and drive. Hebb's theory was too successful; it explained things that seem to be more easily explained by more obvious brain functions.

While the research inspired by Hebb's theory of cell assemblies and Piaget's theory of schemata has been most valuable, it has had to proceed in two contrary directions; instead of avoiding the shortcomings of the two theories, we should confront them directly. This book is an attempt to do just that. It presents a coordination of Hebb's building block theory and of Piaget's black box theory; it is an attempt to take Hebb's theory one level higher and to take Piaget's theory one level lower. I suggest that the two theories meet and firmly bridge the gap between the two approaches to intelligence. I would hope that this coordination has differentiated both theories, made each of them more explicit, more whole, more real, and more understandable. Hebb's theory, I think, gives an understanding of the stages and inner working of Piaget's, and Piaget's theory gives an understanding of the complicated development and behavioral correlates of Hebb's. Finally, Sokolov's research on the orienting and defense responses provides an updating of Hebb's theory and a more sophisticated interpretation of the function of the pain and pleasure centers of the brain as a delicately balanced control between the brain stem (operating system) and the cerebrum (data structure). Sokolov also provides a neural model of Piaget's process of equilibration.

The process of equilibration controls development and function by controlling the variable processing power of the elements in the attention span; this control has been modeled here as a dynamic balance between reverberation (the sum of activity in elements on the attention span, the sum of consequential activity) and total activity of the nervous system; this is a balance between the recognized and the unrecognized, between the known and the unknown, between the certain and uncertain, and, ultimately, a balance between input and output. The process of equilibration and control is a result of the intimate interaction between the growing data structure and the constant operating system, an interaction likened to that in which the changeable, internally stored computer program controls the fixed hardware of the computer, which in turn controls the execution and loading of the program.

The formalized specifications of the data structure and operating system, scattered throughout the second chapter, are not so much statements of fact as simplifications of fact that are necessary to begin thinking and to enable realistic computations in a simulation. In this sense, the formal model of this book represents some progress. Let me state what I think are the most important specifications (without trying to order them by their significance). First is the specification DS7 which insists that the internal data structure and environment must start out (and ultimately be maintained by the rest of the system) such that circular reaction between the nervous system and the environment is possible. Innocent and trivial as this seems, it is the foundation on which all the rest is built. (It is as important as the biochemical requirement that the molecules of our food must have a certain twist to them; the same combinations of atoms but with the wrong twist, as the left hand is a wrongly twisted right hand, would starve us to death.) The continuity and symmetry of the circular reaction between the internal and external worlds is easily overlooked when we theorize about the structure of either world independently of the other. Philosophically, we need to examine more closely this symmetry, continuity, and ultimate unity to understand how the structuring of one world effects the structuring of the other. Second is the specification OS1 which expresses the functional nature of each element of the model. This specification is the most simplified in the model, and the one I suspect will be the most difficult to amplify, depending as it does on the precise nature and structure of the hypothetical cell assembly and the experimentally observed neuron. (I will take this opportunity to be the first to state that I know, absolutely, that each of the specifications of the model are wrong and incomplete; of just how wrong, and just where they are wrong, I am not so sure.) Theoretically, we must know when and how to proceed without such detail. Experimentally, our primitive methods of observation seem too weak and overwhelmed by the complexity of the nervous system to proceed without the strong theoretical direction provided by such obvious gaps. Third, and lumped together here, are the three specifications, OS2, OS5, and OS6, which represent the cognitive reflexes. Together, these define a control process superimposed on the functioning of the cell assemblies. This control is capable of quickly changing the entire nature of the nervous system in a way that depends intimately on the ongoing interaction between nervous system and the environment (or between reverberating assemblies and the nonreverberating assemblies). The cognitive reflexes can quickly change a low attention span system which is, perhaps, producing motor output and changes in the structure of the environment, to a high attention span system which is receiving new information from the environment and recording it as changes in the internal structure. Fourth, and last, is the specification DS8 which defines the exact conditions necessary for learning, and the exact structure of this learning in relation to the old structures. It is the nature of this structured learning that allows the powerful, innate, implicit processes of intelligence to develop and become explicit, observable, and undeniably processes of adult human intelligence.

I should make explicit what has been a helpful misuse, throughout the book, of the formal specifications. This is the complex element. Time and again it has been stated or assumed that a complex of interconnected elements might be treated, for simplicity, as one. (This is the same device used by Hebb to escape the limitations of the building block approach. Where he was careful to call each new level of complexity by a different name, I am insisting here that, in fact, two interconnected complexes of assemblies are much like a single assembly with a different time scale and more complex pattern of activity.) The assumption has been that only scale changes of room on attention span, total activity, and time variables need be made. Otherwise the function, structure, and development of a complex element is defined by the internal structure of more basic elements, and the complex link between two complex elements is simply all the links between subelements (and, hence, complex links may have different strengths). The abstract element may represent a cell assembly, a short term memory or phase cycle, or a concept or cycle of phase cycles; in Piaget's terms, the abstract element or complex of elements may represent a schema. The analysis of structure and substructure need only proceed as far as necessary to explain all the changes in behavior, neuron firing, or whatever observable is being used or inferred: as low as the individual neuron which changes its synaptic connections only when two or more synapses are used simultaneously (DS8?!), or as high as the entire nervous system in metabolic cycles of activity and depression. The informal use of complex elements gives us some understanding of how the process of coordination is the same as the process of differentiation; when several subelements of two different complex elements are coordinated, the coordination also represents a differentiation of the complex elements (differentiation—making only a part of a whole different from the whole by giving that part new connections). Coordination at one level of complexity is the same as differentiation at the next higher level of complexity. To end this summary, I will only mention two more structural concepts that have been used in this book. One is the order of an element, its proximity to the environment; the other is the grouping of elements into self-facilitating groups that can support short term memory and prolonged direction and control of thought and motor activity.

The child never learns anything new, but only coordinates the old; still the child's intellectual capacity is equal to, indeed far outstrips, the intellectual capacity of the adult precisely because the child must (being ignorant) rely entirely on the innate structure, function, and development of intelligence. The adult method of formal abstraction, disciplined thought, and deductive proof of new learning stretch the innate intelligence to its limits while taking the tiniest baby steps in comparison to the strides of insight and creation of which innate intelligence is itself capable. Knowing something of linguistics, I deeply admire the child's intellectual accomplishments and methods; therefore I will imitate them. There is nothing presented in this book that is entirely new, there are no conclusions to be drawn, proofs to be given and defended, or abstractions that are more than a restatement of some concrete images. These would be deductive processes, and this book has been constructed and should be read by an inductive process. The aim is not to know some new facts, but only to understand some old. To give inductive support to the ideas presented here, the more varied the images and interpretations, the better—but only to a point. The aim must also be for conceptual simplicity and not for completeness—some ignorance is necessary for action. I have therefore ranged widely, but not too deeply or thoroughly: just enough to establish an initial connection. As the child knows instinctively, it is better to have an ignorant, but workable and adjustable fantasy (or, more respectably, a model, hypothesis, or theory) than to get lost and paralyzed by the confusion of all the facts; indeed, there are no alternatives. Equilibration (or, more respectably, the scientific method) assures a healthy alternation between learning and action. The child speaks before he has learned the language; I have written this book and a few earlier works from a partial state of ignorance. I have proceeded almost completely by an appropriation and coordination of others' understanding. I make this confession of unoriginality only because I think coordinations are themselves of value; I explain myself so that I can offer this book as a final example of the very process of learning that this book is all about.

REFERENCES

Atkinson, R. C. & Shiffrin, R. M. Human memory: a proposed system and its control processes. In R. W. Spence & J. T. Spence (Eds.), *The psychology of learning and motivation.* Vol. 2. New York: Academic Press, 1967.

Baldwin, J. M. *Mental development.* Norwood, Massachusetts: Norwood Press, 1895.

Bellugi, U. & Brown, R. (Eds.) *The acquisition of language.* Lafayette, Indiana: Child Development Publications, Purdue University, 1964.

Berlyne, D. E. *Conflict, arousal, and curiosity.* New York: McGraw-Hill, 1960.

Bower, T. G. R. The determinants of perceptual unity in infancy. *Psychonomic Science,* 1965, **3,** 323-324.

Bower, T. G. R. Heterogeneous summation in human infants. *Animal Behavior,* 1966, **14,** 395-398.

Bower, T. G. R. The visual world of infants. *Scientific American,* 1966, **215,** 80-92.

Bower, T. G. R. The development of object-permanence: some studies of existence constancy. *Perception and Psychophysics,* 1967, **2,** 411-418.

Bruner, J. S., Oliver, R. R., Greenfield, P. M., *Studies in cognitive growth.* New York: John Wiley & Sons, 1966.

Bruner, J. S. Eye, hand, and mind. In D. Elkind & J. H. Flavell (Eds.), *Studies in cognitive development.* New York: Oxford University Press, 1969.

Charlesworth, W. R. The role of surprise in cognitive development. In D. Elkind & J. H. Flavell (Eds.), *Studies in cognitive development.* New York: Oxford University Press, 1969.

Chomsky, N. In *The acquisition of language.* Lafayette, Indiana: Child Development Publications, Purdue University, 1964. Pp. 35-39.

Chomsky, N. *Aspects of the theory of syntax.* Cambridge, Massachusetts: MIT Press, 1965.

Cunningham, M. A. The implications of developmental psychology for artificial intelligence. Unpublished paper, Univ. of Pennsylvania, 1969.

Cunningham, M. A. The organization of intelligence. *Proceedings of the IEEE Systems Science and Cybernetics Conference,* 1969, 82-89.

Deutsch, J. A. *The structural basis of behavior.* Chicago: University of Chicago Press, 1960.

Dodwell, P. C. A coupling system for coding and learning in shape discrimination. *Psychological Review,* 1964, 71, 148-159.

Estes, W. K. Learning theory and the new "mental chemistry." *Psychological Review,* 1960, 67, 207-223.

Feigenbaum, E. A. & Feldman, J. (Eds.) *Computers and thought.* New York: McGraw-Hill, 1963.

Gorn, S. The individual and political life of information systems. In L. Heilprin, B. E. Markuson, & F. L. Goodwin (Eds.), *Education for information science.* Washington, D. C.: Spartan Books, 1965.

Hebb, D. O. *Organization of behavior.* New York: John Wiley & Sons, 1949.

Hebb, D. O. Drives and the CNS (conceptual nervous system). *Psychological Review,* 1955, 62, 243-254.

Hebb, D. O. The semiautonomous process: its nature and nurture. *American Psychologist,* 1963, 18, 16-27.

Hebb, D. O. Concerning Imagery. *Psychological Review,* 1968, 75, 466-477.

Hockett, C. F. The problem of universals in language. In J. H. Greenberg (Ed.), *Universals of language.* Cambridge, Massachusetts: MIT Press, 1963.

Hubel, D. H., & Wiesel, T. N. Receptive fields, binocular interaction and functional architecture in the cat's visual cortes. *Journal of Physiology,* 1962, 160, 106-154.

Lorente de Nó, R. Analysis of the activity of the chains of internuncial neurons. *Journal of Neurophysiology,* 1938, 1, 207-244.

Mandler, G. Organization and memory. In R. W. Spence & J. T. Spence (Eds.), *The psychology of learning and motivation.* Vol. 1. New York: Academic Press, 1966.

Miller, G. The magical number seven, plus or minus two. *Psychological Review,* 1956, 63, 81-97.

Moreno-Diaz, R. An analytical model of the group 2 ganglion cell in the frog's eye. Instrumentation Laboratory, Massachusetts Institute of Technology, E-1858, October, 1965.

Nilsson, N. J. *Learning machines.* New York: McGraw-Hill, 1965.

Pascual-Leone, J. A mathematical model for the transition rule in Piaget's developmental stages. *Acta Psychologica,* 1970, 32, 301-345.

Pavlov, I. P. *Conditioned reflexes.* London: Oxford University Press, 1927.

Piaget, J. *The language and thought of the child.* New York: World Publishing Co., 1955. First published, 1923.

Piaget, J. *The origins of intelligence in children.* New York: Norton, 1963. First published, 1936.

Piaget, J. *The child's conception of number.* New York: Norton, 1965. First published, 1941.

Piaget, J. *Play, dreams, and imitation in childhood.* New York: Norton, 1962. First published, 1945.

Rosenblatt, F. *Principles of Neurodynamics; perceptions and the theory of brain mechanisms.* Washington, D. C.: Spartan Books, 1962.

Salapatec, P. Visual scanning of triangles by the human newborn. *Journal of Experimental Child Psychology,* 1966, 3, 155-167.

Salapatec, P. Visual scanning of geometric figures by the human newborn. *Journal of Comparative and Physiological Psychology,* 1968, 66, 247-258.

Sokolov, Y. N. *Perception and the conditioned reflex.* Oxford: Pergamon Press, 1963.

Thompson, R. F. *Foundations of physiological psychology.* New York: Harper and Row, 1967.

Vygotsky, L. S. *Thought and language.* Cambridge, Massachusetts: MIT Press, 1962.

Weir, R. H. *Language in the crib.* The Hague: Mouton, 1962.

Wolff, P. H. Observations on the early development of smiling. In B. M. Foss (Ed.), *Determinants of infant behaviour.* Vol. 2, New York: John Wiley & Sons, 1961.

SUBJECT INDEX

A

Accommodation, *see also* Assimilation,
      Equilibration
   functional, 25
   interaction of assimilation and, 114
   motor equivalence, 55
   Piaget's description, 6-7
   in reflex activity, 20
   structural, 25
Activity
   brain function, 129-132
   of input elements, 14
   neurophysiological definition, 9-10
   of output elements, 14
   represented by real numbers, 14
   summation of, 17
   transformation of, 135
Amygdala, 129, 132
Anticipation, 38-39, 56, 123
Assembly, *see* Cell assembly

Assimilation, *see also* Accommodation,
      Equilibration
   functional, 25
   Piaget's description, 6-7
   recognition, 27
   structural, 25
Atkinson, R. C., 97
Attention span, *see also* Orienting response,
      Defense response
   brain mechanisms, 131-132
   control by cognitive reflexes, 19-20
   data structure complexity limited by, 58
   in formal model, 17
   maturation of, 25-26
   minimum necessary for Stage IV, 52
   motor control, 110
   phasic changes, 18
   rate of learning affected by, 124-126
   respiratory effects, 107
   variations in linguistic performance,
      148-150
Auditory and vocal system, 82-86
Avoidance, 105

W